AF799913

Riskless entrepreneurship

Miguel Najul

All rights reserved
The reproduction or translation of any part of this work beyond what is permitted by section 107 or 108 of the Copyright Act of the United States of 1976, which is done without the permission of the copyright owner It is illegal. The request for permission or additional information should be addressed to the author.
This publication is designed to provide accurate and reliable information on the subject covered. It is sold under the understanding that the author is not committed to the results of applying the suggested management technique.

Published by Miguel Najul
Graphic design: Andrea Ochoa
Correction: Ingrid Rodríguez
Cover design: Cristina Solé
Translation: Cory Zacharia and Gabriel Andari
Cover graphics vector: Freepick
Printed by Create Space and sold by Amazon, other distributors, and libraries.

Najul, Miguel
Riskless entrepreneurship / Miguel Najul 2nd edition. United States, 2023
135 pages

ISBN: 978-1-7337392-4-5
Certificate of registration: TXU-2-080-926. Dec 21st, 2017
Risk, risk control, entrepreneurship, new business, planning, evaluation, management, decision making, business plan, business idea, business promotion, ENTREPREVIEW®

On your behalf, my dear Olga

Acknowledgments

I thank my dear Michelle Marie for devoted her time and support me in authoring this book and designing the subsequent work platform. I soon hope to give back such support during her professional development.

I also want to thank the following people for their talent and effort to improve this project: my friends Ingrid Rodríguez, Cory Zacharia, Gabriel Andari, and Cristina Sole.

Finally, I give recognition to all those students, clients, and partners who taught me. It was from them that I learned what I am presenting here, and it is to them that I also pay tribute by presenting this modest essay.

Foreword

I wrote this short prologue because I have enjoyed this book. Not only because it really explains concepts I supposed to have understood throughout my teaching and professional careers. The way to relate two concepts not formally linked before has also been quite a surprise.

The author contextualizes them aptly to make us understand two compelling principles to those who start a business. On the one hand, risk must be the factor to consider when we determine our enterprise's feasibility. On the other, our business risk ends up being our entire responsibility.

These conclusions are based on the perspective of presenting the concept of risk, for which the author suggests differentiating the cause from the effect. This original point of view replaces the old risk classification based on three families that make difficult to identify risks, proposing instead to detect sources of risk considering their potential effects on each business area.

This proposal serves as the conceptual base for measuring risk method, turned into a web-based tool (ENTREPREVIEW), capable of evaluating any entrepreneurship. It says a lot about the quality of the theoretical proposal, but also of the author's enterprising spirit.

I confess I had an adverse reaction to the utopian title of the book. Indeed, it is a marketing slogan, but it can also seem a misleading offer. I recall from my last conversation with the author the following word: "This utopia should be understood as a good purpose, more than a formal objective." Once I turned this page, I reiterate my congratulations to this experienced professor, and I invite you to enjoy, as I did, this original and well-presented work.

Prof. Bautisto Hernandez

Entrepreneur

Contents

Chapter 1. Introduction

By proposing an original approach to classic topics, we aim to add skills to the readers' performance.

We use as title "Riskless Entrepreneurship" to highlight the condition that ideally, any good business endeavor should achieve. We propose this perspective because risk determines the feasibility of our initiative and forces us to keep it under control from the very moment, we take over the planning process.

When referring to the entrepreneurship process itself, control can be exercised in ways that will reduce the omissions or errors that can negatively impact the reliability of our analyses and conclusions. Control also, steers us towards a strategy that mitigates or avoids those sources of risk that can spark unwanted events in the latter stages of our business.

As a product of this strategy, the reliability of our entrepreneurship will not just only depend on the accuracy of the data obtained or the quantitative technique that transforms the data into results and value. It will also depend on the consistency between the collected information about the business and its real potentials within the environments that affect it. This change of focus suggests the elaboration of a "reliable business proposal," which ultimately depends on the control of the risk sources that will always be latent in our projects.

To visualize the omnipresence of risk in promoting any business, we have organized this text into seven chapters. They start by setting forth the basic definitions of how to understand risks, and by suggesting a workplan to set up a business.

Although the concepts we present are easily understandable, putting them into practice requires the simultaneous application of analysis and managerial techniques, which add complexity to the task. For this, we have designed case studies that require time to be fully assimilated. However, we are sure that dedication will be rewarded when readers learn how to apply the proposed techniques.

We wish that this first version will accomplish our goal. Not only by spreading theoretical and practical knowledge. We also hope that in the future, readers will explore business ideas with full awareness of the existing risks[1].

---

1 We have reviewed at least sixty books and over three hundred publications, articles and working papers about this subject. Since this book is not for the author's academic ladder promotion, we refer to the best and accessible sources for readers.

1.1 Going into entrepreneurship

A new business venture is widely understood as a job alternative that covers our standard of living with the added advantage of being the owners of our time and destiny. "No more bosses or unfair work's schedule... simply more freedom to manage priorities without having to answer to anyone while enjoying a more balanced personal life" [2]

Unfortunately, those who have undertaken any entrepreneurial activity know that this adventure does not begin or end like that. Instead, entrepreneurship is usually a very intensive process that takes much of our time and energy. Frequently, it can make us slaves to a project without reaping rewards for the risks we take.

Longevity

In 2009, 49% of active businesses in the United States had been in business for 10 years or more. 24% had between 4 and 9 years of operation and the remaining 27% had less than 4 years of life.

Given the obstacles and problems we usually find in an enterprise, we ask ourselves, why do we get involved in such an endeavor? What compels us to seek a complicated path to our personal and professional development? Would be making the mistake of overestimating our capabilities?

These ideas have always intrigued me. Even more today when entrepreneurship has exploded all over the media. It probably is the most promoted activity worldwide since many agents and investors have discovered an exciting niche for promotion and doing business.

The concept has proven so attractive that even politicians now include it as part of their campaigns promises, openly offering incentives and resources to new enterprises. Thus, entrepreneurship has become a slogan of progress that, unfortunately, will not benefit everyone.

Despite all the above, we welcome its promotion because many discover new ways of developing professionally and financially. Therefore, a growing number of institutions and professional groups are offering information, services, and even specialized help in this matter.

---

2 We coined the expression from many entrepreneurs when explaining the reasons why they undertake new businesses.

Nevertheless, much of this promotion can be quite deceptive, since all these entities encourage new enterprises without mentioning the thousands of people who fail for different reasons. In fact, the "mortality rate" of new businesses is much higher than its success rate[3], which suggests that entrepreneurship is not for everyone, even if the opposite is touted.

During the 2005-2012 period, a training program for entrepreneurs took place[4]. There, a module on "Risk Control" surfaced and it turned out to be a real experiment. Until then, the topic had only been applied to corporations and was treated using very complex analytics language and tools. For this reason, it was necessary to adapt the content, using both a more straightforward style that would allow explaining the concepts and tools, and presenting examples that entrepreneurs would relate to.

This experience not only allowed learning about a very particular world, full of wrongly understood rules and myths. It also allowed getting to know more about new businesses, thanks to the wide variety of projects.

Additionally, I gathered data through a survey[5] designed to research critical entrepreneurial subjects, such as financing and partnerships. Some results were in line with expectations. For example, those surveyed overwhelmingly affirmed (90.8%) that they preferred to establish a company with partners, especially those who could contribute with capital, as well as business experience (78%). This trend was stronger among participants who had less business experience (i.e., employees and students).

Likewise, results showed that 63% of those participants had preferences for financing their projects through a combination of debt and capital. This group proposed, on average, a debt-capital proportion of 45%/55%, which was a very generous ratio regarding the local banking standards for financing new enterprises at that time.

---

3 Entrepreneurship and the U.S. Economy. Bureau of Labor Statistic. http://www.bls.gov/bdm/entrepreneurship/bdm_chart3.htm

4 Program for Entrepreneurs, Institute of Studies of Administration IESA. Caracas Venezuela. www.iesa.edu.ve

5 The survey was answered by 120 entrepreneurs using a questionnaire based on 11 questions, with nominal answers. All questions were multiple choice or semi-open type. 100% of respondents belong to the socio-economic sectors A, B, and C + that represent, aprox 15.5% of the country's population. 89% had work experience, and the rest were undergraduate and graduate students.

A surprising 55% of those surveyed suggested that they would ideally set up companies with three or more partners, a result that was greater among those entrepreneurs with less business experience. This portion was notable because respondents did not consider the challenges of managing companies via third parties in a country where mutuality is not part of the business culture.

As we mentioned before, the survey could detect some missing concepts regarding crucial variables in the development of the enterprises. For example, over half of the entrepreneurs (52%) would not opt for bank financing, to avoid formalities and conditions required by financial institutions when lending. Moreover, a quarter of those surveyed (26.1%) affirmed that personal funds were cheaper than those offered by banks, and a somewhat lesser portion (20.7%) indicated that self-financing lowers the bankruptcy risk.

As we can see, there is a lot to understand about entrepreneur's comprehension of these and other critical aspects. Therefore, it seems there is a need to prepare practical teaching tools able to clarify the concepts required for starting a new business.

1.2 Why consider Risk Control?

We are talking about teaching because this is the primary goal of this text. In it, we organize the necessary steps that precede any business decision. Then we explain the role played by each piece of the puzzle in planning a venture. In this manner, the reader will not only have an exhaustive work guide to adopt when starting a business. The idea is also to understand the consequences of each omission made during the entrepreneurship process.

Risk sources

42.1% of US active companies in 2013, closed during 2014 due to lack of money

For this presentation, we chose the perspective offered by Risk Control because business developments are very prone to failure due to weaknesses that founders do not foresee.

We can state that such vulnerabilities arise because of a lack of resources (e.g., personnel, monetary, management). As we know, at first, entrepreneurs usually work with less than the essentials. Then, while developing the business idea, they gradually get the resources which allow them to carry their project forward. During this process, entrepreneurs need to identify what is or is not a priority. It will allow getting the essential resources to mitigate, if not avoid, the risks that might affect the business performance.

Risk Control is the discipline that complements planning in this very crucial aspect of the business. It reveals the vulnerable side of the enterprise and helps us understand why it is not possible to achieve goals, given the existing weaknesses. To this end, this discipline identifies and measures the potential impact of the risk factors, simultaneously helping find work formulas to mitigate their effects.

That is why this text includes chapters dedicated to the topic of risk. We explain its origins, the forms it takes, and its possible effects. Then we propose practical ways of controlling it. It is not a banal proposition that improve the reader's general culture. Instead, it aims to clarify what the risks are and what are the differences among their causes and effects.

Once explained this criterion, it becomes easier for entrepreneurs to identify potential problems they may face. It will also help to create a working outline that makes it possible to manage resource shortages and consequently adjust the goals and objectives of the project.

There is no better management discipline for achieving this understanding of a project. Indeed, the experience I gained during the workshops showed me that Risk Control emerged as a surprise for many of the participants. Not only because of the number of duties and subjects that required their attention suddenly increased. Likewise, risks identification spurred many entrepreneurs to reconsider their work plans, as well as the scope and nature of their projects.

Given this valuable experience, I decided to write Riskless Entrepreneurship. Not only as a means of orderly collecting the ideas that revolve around the Risk Control of a new project. The idea is also to spread a practical approach that will be useful to every business entrepreneur.

1.3 Our Focus

Traditionally, we understand entrepreneurship as the stage that converts an idea into an ongoing business. Its duration and complexity are highly variable, as it depends on the type of business, the access to necessary resources, and the dedication of the entrepreneurs.

Even though other publications present similar criteria, we have here somewhat reordered the topic defining critical points in its organization and initiation. Thus, we have divided the stage that precedes the operation into two different phases: strategic and pre-operation.

The strategic phase begins with the idea of a project and ends when entrepreneurs formally establish a company with the duly funding. The pre-operation phase, on the other hand, begins with the acquisition of the resources required for the planned operation and completes when the first sale of the product or service takes place[6].

As mentioned, the object of our study is the strategic phase, and for this reason, we review the processes that compose it. As we will see, these processes seek to determine the project's viability, which depends on both the return promised by the business activity and the ways to finance the required investment.

Resolving the latter aspects involves a series of complex and furthermore interdependent studies, analyses, and calculations. Given the difficulty involved, we present and explain an archetype of the strategic exercise, so that it can serve as the guide which will enable the fulfillment of this critical phase.

For this proposal, Risk Control is the connecting thread since we suggest an appropriate control of each analysis and exercise. The idea is to avoid gaps in the information to consider when deciding the fate of the new business. Similarly, Risk Control is involved in the planning process itself when identifying the resources to operate the business dependably.

In such manner, entrepreneurs should have explicit references on how to carry out a risk analysis of the project. The idea here is to offer a simplified procedure better adjusted to the conditions the entrepreneur will face when organizing a business. Consequently, we omitted, for example, quantitative control techniques because during the entrepreneurship phase, such methods might be useless[7].

---

6 This outline has exceptions. Such is the case of real estate projects whose operation are based on building a property that can be sold before, during, or after finishing the work.

7 A difficult topic to decide. We chose not to include quantitative techniques usually recommended for planning and risk control, as they are useless to analyze businesses lacking historical information.

Despite our effort to offer a simple explanation of this entrepreneurial process, we must not conclude that planning and Risk Control are trivial matters. Indeed, some complications demand from entrepreneurs, knowledge, and experience of different management disciplines. They must be aware that setting up a business requires, among other skills, studying the market, defining the consumer, planning the operation, working out budgets, forecasting results and setting the value of the enterprise. In summary, entrepreneurship ends up being the equivalent of an M.B.A., entirely applied.

Paradoxically, entrepreneurs must put a good number of management disciplines into practice, even without knowing them. Of course, it is always possible to obtain help of specialists in those areas where we know little. Unfortunately, access to this expertise is limited because entrepreneurs rarely have financial resources to pay for such support. That is why entrepreneurs end up incorrectly applying many management techniques, or ignoring them altogether, thus leading them to make high-risk decisions.

Because this ambiguity is prevalent among entrepreneurs, we have written "Riskless Entrepreneurship." Not only as a decalogue for carrying out a work plan designed to determine the feasibility of a project. But also, as a guide for those who have little of an idea about the demands of the entrepreneurship process. We hope this text will help you make wise business decisions, either for carrying out attractive projects or for discarding initiatives, difficult to profit from.

1.4 ENTREPREVIEW®

As stated, this book presents a method for controlling the planning, evaluation, and decision-making processes involved in the entrepreneurship stage. All these processes require the design and management of an important number of tables, lists, and matrixes that make it possible to classify and interrelate data and information.

Given the complexity of the procedures, we have created a web-based platform named "ENTREPREVIEW®." This platform automates access to a group of surveys adjusted to different businesses. Based on the progress attained in the entrepreneurship process, it is possible to determine the risk level derived from the omissions or inconsistencies.

Since this is a free service platform, we suggest you visit and use it, taking into consideration that the implicit entrepreneurial model is discussed in this book. Thereby, users can learn guidelines to carry out this planning phase, while getting a diagnosis for the reliability of the work they have done.

Do not hesitate to use the platform, especially if you have taken the time to read this book. Unfortunately, we cannot guarantee the success of your initiative. Nevertheless, we believe that the diagnosis is going to be useful to complete a work plan that enables you to take care rapidly and efficiently of the potential sources of risk.

1.5 Further editions

We hope to offer soon an influential book, that not only includes a better explained proposal. We also plan to include in the next editions a set of statistics of the entrepreneurships analyzed through ENTREPREVIEW®.

There is a lot to understand about the entrepreneurship world and it seems we are on the right track in getting information from the right source. The workshops and courses given have already allowed us to identify and prioritize the entrepreneurs' fears and flaws. We now have a vast field to collect evidence from and to identify patterns that help entrepreneurs make less emotional business decisions.

At present, programs sponsored by public policy makers, investment entities and academia are not being effective since the mortality rate of new businesses remains high. We must then double down on our work to share information and experiences, which allows us to better understand the relevant factors in creating new businesses.

For now, we offer this modest essay with no-profit expectation. Thereby, we will start spreading a subject that is complex, but also essential to those involved in creating new businesses.

Chapter 2.
Understanding risks

If we understand the concept of risk and the origin of this condition, it will be easier to control it.

One of the most frequent mistakes in dealing with risks is to confuse the cause with the effect. Even though this error is avoidable, it is also excusable since much of the specialized literature identifies risks inconsistently, ignoring details that seem just formalities, but are actually not.

As a matter of fact, the most popular way to identify risks is by pointing out the area, operation, or activity in which the event might occur. Therefore, the "risk of default" arises, for example, when a borrower loses the ability to repay a financial commitment[8].

Credit risk source

Credit risk often has operational shortcomings behind it. In fact, the risk's source in a credit operation does not lie in the borrowers' financial condition, but on the lender's inability to determine the default likelihood.

Likewise, liquidity risks are related to the difficulty that may arise when trading securities in illiquid markets, while personnel risks are related to the inconveniences to put into practice an appropriate human resource management policy, (e.g., discrimination or failure to comply with formal duties as an employer).

It also happens that risks are identified through a specific environment (i.e., contexts), that could affect the business progress (e.g., political, or social risks).

Finally, risks are also identified according to the effect they can produce on the business (e.g., legal risks or reputational risks) [9]

Popularity of these modalities to identify risk is consistent with the classification based on "families" (i.e., credit, market and operational)[10] mostly used by international organizations. Despite their vast diffusion and use, these classifications produce decoys that complicate risk management.

Contrary to this proposal, here we will focus on understanding the differences between cause and effect. As we will prove, this perspective makes it easier to manage risk.

---

8 http://www.investinganswers.com/financial-dictionary/bonds/default-risk-1313
9 http://deloitte.wsj.com/riskandcompliance/2013/10/02/why-reputational-risk-is-a-strategic-risk/
10 Basel Committee on Banking Supervision. Consultative Document. Overview of The New. Basel Capital Accord. Issued for comment by 31 May 2001. January. http://www.bis.org/bcbs/

This fresh approach focuses on the conditions that create weaknesses and, subsequently, the derived effects. To adopt this approach, we will use terms such as losses, areas, sources of risk, and contexts which help us comprehensively define risks.

Later, we will present a tool that allows handling the elements mentioned above. At this point, we refer to the Risk Matrix, which is nothing more than tables, figures or graphs that organize the information obtained from the different sources of risk.

It is useful to have these graphic resources at hand, since the idea of the management risk control is to identify, measure, and rank risks, to then define corrective actions. For this purpose, matrices make it easier to classify and plan, as they help us gather and correlate the information obtained from each source of risk.

2.1 What is Risk?

Let us begin by defining what risk is and what it is not. Thus, risk is the condition of an activity performed with a set of resources whose lack of quality, quantity, or sufficiency can lead to equity losses.

Vulnerability condition (examples)

- Few staff to serve customers
- Lack of procedure to control a fire accident
- No maintenance of cargo vehicles
- Computer network obsolescence

To fully understand this concept, we should focus on three elements included in the definition. The first is the "condition," a term that illustrates a state or set of situations, constraints, and/or deficiencies of the activity we perform.

This mix of factors, through which it is possible to define aspects of an activity and identifies elements that explain the vulnerability that exposes us to undesirable events.

The second term refers to the "resources." Precisely, the availability and condition of them determine the vulnerability of the activity that we accomplish.

Theoretically, if resources are available according to the quality, quantity, and capacity required, then it will be possible to reduce/avoid failures or events that can lead to the losses we are trying to avoid. If we do not take care of these conditions, then the business may operate poorly, even achieving the expected results, but exposing itself to events that may affect any of its areas or outcomes.

The last element refers to the "company's equity." Let us remember that one of the management objectives is not just to exploit the business to obtain profits. It is also necessary to avoid losses, tangible or not, that may also affect the company's equity.

Not a risk (examples)

- A possibility
- A lost
- An external incident
- An unplanned event
- A pessimistic scenario
- A negative business context

Although this is not the traditional definition, it does not explain risks according to the way of identifying, measuring, or treating them. Risk is simply a condition that we can identify, describe, and even quantify through managerial analysis[11].

2.2 Losses

Let's start by defining a "source of risk" as the starting point of a chain of incidents whose origin is a weakness. When such weakness is not duly addressed, it usually affects the related areas because of its potential to produce events that can cause losses that affect our business equity (Figure 2.1).

Figure 2.1
Sequence that explain the losses that may impact equity.

To understand how weakness, deficiencies, and events are produced, just remember that companies have to attend many responsibilities (i.e., areas). Therefore, it will be necessary to use multiple resources (e.g., human, technological, physical).

When organizing the business, management assigns resources to each area, persuaded that these resources will be sufficient for the scale and complexity of the pending tasks.

11 Please read; https://en.wikipedia.org/wiki/Risk .

When this assignment is wrong, or there are no possibilities for obtaining the quality and quantity of resources necessary to operate safely, we will have deficiencies that, to a greater or lesser extent, diminish the business operating capacity.

Deficiencies

Deficiencies do not respond to any specific pattern. They simply exist when an activity is carried out beyond its resources' capacities

Note that weaknesses will give rise to deficiencies, omissions or errors, both in operation and in the way of generating information. Usually, these deficiencies are detected on time, allowing management to decide if they live with them or fix them as soon as they can.

There are situations, however, when deficiencies are not identified or mitigated. That prevents the business from fully complying with either a duty or an objective. When such situations arise, anticipated or not, we are at a risk condition that is subject to an "event." The consequence deriving from any of the events that happen over time is called "Impact," which is nothing more than a "loss" for the company.

As stated in Figure 2.2, businesses can lose in several ways, because of certain events. Namely: money, market share, fixed assets, profitability, and fines or penalties. Whatever the loss, this will cause a further impact, either on the company's image, or on its capacity to produce cash flow, or on both elements at the same time. Whatever that subsequent impact is, there will always be an adverse effect on the equity's value.

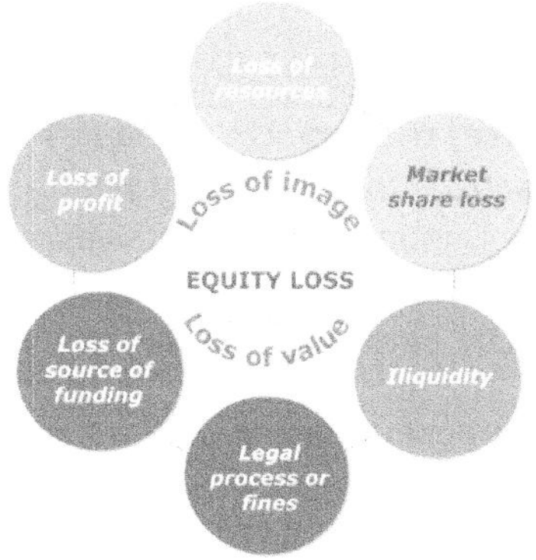

Figure 2.2
Families of impacts derived from the weaknesses or shortcomings.

This relation between weakness, deficiencies, events, and losses can be easily illustrated when we analyze events of relative importance, in which several losses occur at the same time with the inevitable result of affecting the equity value.

It would be the case of the dairy food distributor Fonterra (New Zealand), which because of the lack of control in its production line (Weakness), delivered in August 2013 a batch of bacteria contaminated milk cream (deficiency) that could cause botulism and other complications in the consumers' health[12].

¿? Critical areas

Can we quantify all losses in monetary terms? If so, how do we account impacts on the company image, whose problems are public domain?

The first effect from this failure was a notorious public reaction (Event 1), which exerted an immediate pressure on the corporation's board. Despite senior management initially denying the problem, the case quickly escalated to government entities (Event 2), given the importance of this company in the export of dairy products from New Zealand to the rest of the world.

The economic effects materialized immediately since the country's exports of dairy products were stopped, causing losses to Fonterra and many others in this sector (Impact 1). The market was affected since regular customers turned to other producers (Impact 2) who had lower production volumes. This resulted in an imbalance between supply and demand, causing a price hike for this commodity (Impact 3).[13]

This case illustrates how a weakness (operational) can affect a company in different ways. Of course, the impacts spread, among other reasons, because the event reached the public's opinion, creating a chain reaction. But aside from this catastrophe, it was possible to detect a series of incidents (i.e., weakness, deficiencies, events, and losses) as well as the effect caused by each event on the company's equity.

For our small business' purpose, it is unnecessary to suffer catastrophes to address our weaknesses. Less severe deficiencies must also be addressed, and for this, we also need to identify the cause-effect

12 https://www.cnbc.com/id/100938448
13 http://www.nasdaq.com/markets/milk.aspx

relationship and understand the consequence that can ultimately be generated.

To illustrate this connection in everyday problems, we present in Table 2.3 examples on how different sources of risk (not addressed), produce deficiencies (may or may not be clear), that facilitate the occurrence of events that may generate losses of different magnitude and nature [14].

SOURCES OF RISK (EXAMPLES)	DEFICIENCIES (EXAMPLES)	EVENTS (EXAMPLES)	CONSECUENCES (Potential)
Lack of a comprehensive accounting application Lack of a market study No team to collect receivables accounts	Lack of control of purchases and inventories There is no a realistic pricing structure Seller's discretionary handle of collections	Over/Under-supply of raw material Ups and downs in sales and production Non-scheduled accounts receivable's hikes	LIQUIDITY LOSS
Unethical behavior Formal duties unknowing Information gaps in systems	Promote rigged/biased agreements Delay in tax return filing Lack of information protection	Lawsuits Tax fines Scam for information hacking	LEGAL PROCESSES, FINES OR PENALTIES
No experience planning business No business strategies No procedure to buy supplies	Lack/incomplete investment budget No business value Lack of agreements with suppliers	Over/Under-supply of vital resources Restriction to create a partnership No credit from suppliers	FUNDING LOSS
Lack of maintenance schedule Lack of surveillance and security Weak HHRR management	Fails in equipment and machines No protection of facilities Low wages and bonuses	Non-scheduled production outages Vandalism and theft High staff turnover	LOSS OF ASSETS, EMPLOYEES AND OTHER RESOURCES
No test lab Lack of cost accounting Lack of operational planning	Absence of quality control Undetermined operating margin No guidelines for restock inventories	High rate of product returns Inaccurate income statement Insufficient production volume	LOSS OF PROFITS
Obsolete machinery No sales manager No marketing management	Restrictions to change packaging Poor distribution channels Out-of-Market price structure	No adaptation to customer demand Delayed or deliveries failures Insufficient sales	SHARE MARKET LOSS

Table 2.3
Consequences from deficiencies
caused by different sources of risk (Examples)

Consider the multiple links and interdependencies in this set of examples. As we can see, a specific source of risk can generate several events, as it occurs, for instance, with the inability to plan any of the business areas.

Such failure cannot only limit the operations and sales. It can also mean, for example, insufficient financing.

Different deficiencies may also lead to the same consequence. It occurs when sales goals cannot be reached, because of production problems or the incorrect pricing of the product.

Additionally, the same loss can result from different events. It is the case for companies whose profits diminish because of a wrong definition

[14] Consequences can always be organized according to the losses families (consequences) presented in Diagram 2.2

of their niche market, and also by unscheduled increases in their production costs.

As we can see, correlations between weaknesses, deficiencies, events, and impacts are manifold, which is not an anecdotal issue. Indeed, these relationships force us to be rigorous when analyzing the sources of risks.

> **¿? More about image**
>
> For small or medium-sized companies, what is the management unit that takes care of the company's image?. If we refer a large company, there would be a different unit?

Note that the exercise for determining potential problems is not complete with the simple identification of the deficiencies that arise from some sources of risk. It will also be necessary to consider the likely events derived from them, as well as the multiple impacts that such deficiencies may cause on the company's equity.

It not only allows us to understand the vulnerability of our operation but also enables the ranking of the existing deficiencies ordered by importance. This facilitates the definition of an action plan to help minimize them according to the available resources[15].

2.3 Areas

The second element to consider when identifying risks is the set of "Areas". They represent the universe of activities and processes that allow the business to achieve its objectives and fulfill its mission. Thus, Areas are all those mandatory tasks for the business to accomplish its purpose.

For Risk Control purpose, an Area represents the place, time, opportunity or activity where may be weaknesses that give rise to one or more events occurrence.

It is essential to identify the Areas because they offer precise coordinates to locate the business' weak points[16]. It makes the planning

---

15 Various terms used here are new for readers. Therefore, we invite you to pay extra attention to them, to correctly identify potential problems in business. We present some examples at the end of this chapter, and we provide more information in chapter six, where we consider the cause-effect relationship discussed here.

16 This does not mean that the scope will determine the type of risk, as was commented at the beginning of the chapter. It is simply one more variable that helps to identify and locate risk.

and budgeting processes more efficient when assign the resources needed to mitigate the potential weaknesses.

Figure 2.4 shows the different Areas of a typical organization. As seen, Areas are identified by "functions" (e.g., financial operations, market compliance) instead of management or functional units (e.g., Human Resources Department, Administration).

Figure 2.4
Common areas of any organization

This makes it easier to detect the sources of risk, either in those areas shared by several functional units or in a process that depends on more than one management[17]. This increases the controls effectiveness by integrating all those functional units, directly or indirectly, related to each scrutinized process.

In this classification, areas are not specific enough to guide us to the identification of weaknesses. To convert this classification into a practical work map, we must establish a sub-classification that more accurately identifies the typical activities or processes that make up each family[18].

---

17 A product manufacturing is a good example of processes that demand simultaneous or sequential participation of different units (e.g., warehouse, production, quality control, packaging and shipping)

18 See an example of this classification in Attachment C Use the list presented to prepare a map of your business areas, to orderly complete the risk's sources identification.

Thus, "Administration and Control" Area includes, among other activities, the "Accounting and financial registry of operations". Within this subset, we may include the creation and administration of the "Accounts Code", the "Operation Accounting Registry", as well as the "Management of documents, invoices, and contracts".

Note that the above criterion applies not only to developed companies. They are also valid for the very beginning enterprises, despite they are small organizations without all the previously identified areas.

Remember that partners care to collect, analyze and process information in the strategic phase to decide the future of the business. Accordingly, Figure 2.5 organizes the processes comprising this phase that work as the actual areas of the strategic exercise.

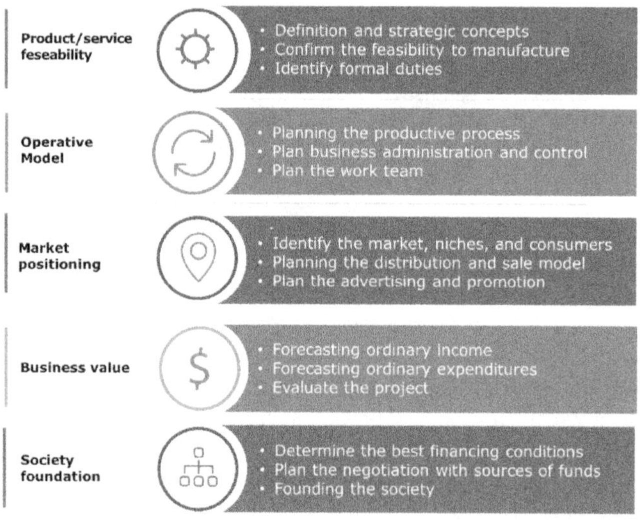

Figure 2.5
List of the processes (areas) that make up the strategic phase, distributed by goals. Example: Manufacturing company.

As noted, none of these areas is operational. Namely, they do not produce, nor buy resources, or provide a service. Here, it is fundamental to investigate, plan, and evaluate. However, risk control applies because all strategic phase areas are shelters of weaknesses that will affect both the rest of the exercises that take place in this phase and the setup and operation of the future business (i.e., pre operational phase and so on).

2.4 Resources

Resources are all those means (e.g., assets, employees, rights, ideas, organization and even licenses) available for the business to perform its ordinary and extraordinary operations. For methodological purposes, we classify them into four families: Personal, Organization, Information, and Assets.

Their description, as well as a list of the typical resources comprised in each family, are shown in Table 2.6.

PERSONNEL	ORGANIZATION	INFORMATION	ASSETS
All human resources (internal and external) that perform functions (direct or indirect) that contribute with company objectives	Any resource that helps the staff to fulfilling effectively their responsibilities.	Resources that produce, modify and distribute the information that supports management decisions, duties complies and keep the organization informed	All tangible and intangible resources, not included in the previous groups, which are also necessary to carry out the operations and activities
• Management Shareholders, Board of Directors, CEO • Staff Managements, employees and workers • Others Outsourcing, providers, advisors	• Planning Business model, Goals/objectives • Standards and procedures Procedures, Tech instructions • Organization Formal structure, Organizational climate • Management/ supervisors Incentives & promotions Management controls	• Information and reports Studies and researches, Operations records • Systems Operative systems, App, Database Communications, Internet, Intranet • Equipment Computers, servers, networks, peripherals	• Financial assets Cash, securities, debts, receivables • Real estate Buildings, warehouse, offices, lands, plots • Intangible assets Licenses, rights, Insurance policies • Fixed assets Machinery, tools • Inventories Raw Material, supplies, Finished goods

Table 2.6
Description and example of families' business resources

When you carefully check this classification, it is possible to detect two conditions regarding how we define the resources. On the one hand, they do not have to be "owned" by the business. When considering them "available," we are not discarding that they can legally belong, and even be managed by third parties.

Here, we refer to those that provide inputs or services (e.g., Outsourcings, suppliers, partner companies), that ultimately bring capacity/quality to the operation.[19]

[19]Just as these suppliers reinforce or simply serve part of our areas, their sources of risk could affect the performance of our company.

On the other hand, resources do not always have an assigned value in the business' accounting. Under this concept, we may include intangible resources such as guidelines, technical instructions, organizational model, and any other elements that are, directly or indirectly, being used by the business to meet its objectives.

Keep in mind, that we are considering the resources in our analysis because they are strongly related to the Risks to operate every business area. Only available resources should allow accomplishing goals and objectives in the safest way possible.

For such a "security condition" to exist, resources must be available in sufficient quantity and quality. Additionally, resources must fulfil other conditions (Table 2.7) intrinsic to their nature, and the role to play in the business.

PERSONNEL

QUALIFIED: Employees must have the formal education and experience to exercise the assigned position. The organization must develop an induction process to induce on employees what is expected of them.

SUFFICIENT: Each activity or process must be executed by a number of employees that guarantee the objectives fulfillment according to the budget and established time frame.

COMMITTED: In order to avoid disloyalties, the organization must align the employee's commitment to the corporate objectives and mission. For this, it is necessary to design policies that reward loyalty and good work, while encouraging ethical behavior.

WELL MANAGED: In all organizations, top management should act as an organizer and controller of the regular processes and activities. For this, staff must be duly assigned to perform every task that comprised each functional area.

ORGANIZATION

RELEVANT: Standards must exist to indicate the conditions to well-perform processes and business activities. Technical instructions, guidelines and norms show the employee how to perform task and activities effectively and safely.

SIMPLE: Beyond the technical specifications of every activity, rules must be simple and clearly worded, to avoid doubts and uncertainties for the employee when performing or supervise tasks.

UPDATED: It is necessary that the organization invests resources and permanent attention to keep norms, guidelines and standards updated. Delays could disqualify them as a source of consultation, but also as a valid reference to evaluate procedures and results.

COMMUNICATED: The purpose of a standard is to guarantee results by complying with certain procedures and conditions. For this, organizations must focus on disseminating them to avoid self-learning or poor training, that are often causes of expensive events for the organization.

OTHER ASSETS

AVAILABLE: Resources must support the ordinary and extraordinary operations. In addition, resources must be available on time, so that operations do not suffer interruptions or failures.

SUITABLE: Resources should meet technical/managerial/administrative specifications to support the productive, administrative, and financial areas.

MAINTENED: All fixed assets, especially equipment, machinery, and premise must comply with all technical and safety requirements. Regular maintenance plans must reach optimum work conditions.

SAFETY: Security concerns the set of rules and resources to put in place to prevent damage from third parties outside the company. Likewise, security corresponds to the monitoring of the rules that ensure the integrity of assets and personnel.

INFORMATION

AVAILABLE: Systems components must guarantee the storage, protection, and data access.

EFECTIVE: Systems must allow generating relevant information to the entire organization. For this purpose, information delivery must occur timely and consistently.

SAFETY: To manage data and information safely, it is necessary to get resources that avoid unauthorized access or unofficial data distribution.

EFFICIENT: It is critical to manage data and generate productively and economically management information. Compatibility and adopt well-proven solutions may be critical to achieve these goals.

RELIABLE: It is key to access, manage, and produce information according to operational and administrative requirements based on the business management and the legal framework.

INTEGRITY: Information must be accurate to meet business requirements. Accessing the primary sources and storage/protect the database are unconditional for this purpose.

Table 2.7
Must-meet conditions for the resources to operate the business safely

When we refer to the Strategic Phase, there are two ideas regarding Resources, that explain the importance of this initial phase in the business's endowment.

Keep in mind that the Strategic Phase is where information and evidence are collected so we can understand the viability of the business and its attractiveness to those willing to finance it. It is a phase whose fundamental resource is information, and within it, entrepreneurs must plan, as far as possible, all the business development details.

Sources of risk

When we decide on the business to build, we also select the type of risk to face. If the market is volatile, for instance, we must develop mechanisms to foresee its changes. As explained, the market is not the source of risk. It is, indeed, the lack of the mechanisms (i.e., resources) to alert us to the occurrence of unexpected behavior.

In most cases, entrepreneurs do not plan everything, because of lack of information, limited time, lack of experience or money. In these cases, one or more areas will be left without a complete development plan, and this is where the operational weaknesses can germinate, since the required resources may lack in sufficient quality or quantity.

Indeed, there will be weaknesses that can be solved along the way without consequences, such as buying resources required by the administrative activities. However, there are other more complicated areas, that demand preventive attention. Not attending to them in a timely manner can generate considerable effects in other critical activities, such as production or sales.

An example of these cases can be seen in those manufacturing enterprises, whose waste material requires special handling by the city collection service. In these cases, business cannot postpone compliance until starting its operations. If formal procedures are not completed on time, it would lead to a paralysis of the productive process and expose the business to fines and possible closures.

This and other similar cases confirm that planning is essential to provide businesses with the resources to operate with the least possible number of flaws. Despite the budgetary limitations that may exist, entrepreneurs must always plan their operations in full. Remember that there will always be time to address the weaknesses, if and only if we know in advance what they are and how they could affect the business performance.

2.5 Contexts

This is the last element included in the risk identification and represents the set of environments, circumstances, constraints, and conjunctures that surround all of us and, specifically, may affect the business performance.

An option to classify this element is presented in Figure 2.8, where we suggest eight families. They include the environments that, more frequently, are bound to all economic activity. From this approach and the role played by contexts on risks, we point out three important aspects[20].

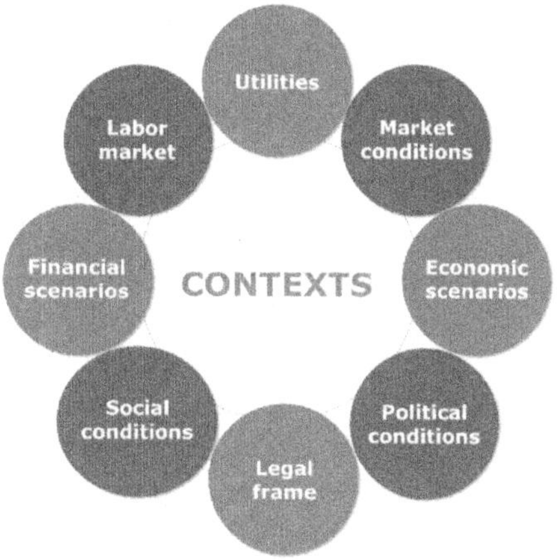

Figure 2.8
Contexts families

On the one hand, it does not matter what location, size, nature, and complexity the business has. Contexts end up being efficient amplifiers or attenuators of existing risk sources. The condition that distinguishes which of the two roles a specific context plays is its "predictability".

In general, the more feasible it is for the managers to predict contexts, the more likely they can prepare a strategy and get the resources to take advantage of them or mitigate their undesirable effects.

20 Other approach is suggested by Erkko Autioa, Martin Kenney, Philippe Mustar, Don Siegel, Mike Wright "Entrepreneurial innovation: The importance of context", journal www.elsevier.com. Mar 2013. https://kenney.faculty.ucdavis.edu/wp-content/uploads/sites/332/2019/12/2014-RP-Entre-preneurial-Innovation-Autio-et-al.pdf

On the other hand, the fact that some events complicate any of the business areas does not turn the Contexts as sources of risk.[21]

Attenuating contexts examples

- Low inflation economy
- Modern infrastructure access
- No trading barriers
- Democratic regime
- Growing economy
- Expansive fiscal policy

As stated, risks depend only on the business vulnerability existing in any of its areas. That is why a business does not need changes in its environment or through extreme situations so that a weakness may arise, and an event occurs, resulting in unexpected losses.

However, considering the Contexts is fundamental, either when determining the potential success of a line of business operating under specific conditions, or when looking for answers to external conditions that may affect the business performance.

In order to handle these variables, keep in mind that contexts are usually interdependent from the moment in which the behavior of an environment depends on, but also changes, the evolution of other environments. The classic example of this interdependence can be seen between the social and the economic contexts. Similar good economic conditions promote an improvement in people's welfare, but a deterioration in the social conditions would reduce the willingness of economic agents to make investments that can significantly increase economic activity.

Amplifying contexts examples

- Very competitive markets
- High volatility in supplies costs
- Foreign exchange restrictions
- Political turmoil environment

This relationship between two or more environments must be considered when we elaborate complex scenarios to realistically forecast based on the data collected.

In these cases, entrepreneurs not only must assure that variables represent the contexts. There must also be consistency among all the Contexts considered, according to a logical relation between the market, the economy, and the country where the business is being developed.[22]

---

21 Managing Strategic Surprise: Lessons from Risk Management & Risk Assessment. Paul Bracken, Ian Bremmer and David Gordon. Cambridge Edition, Cambridge University Press, 2008. ISBN 0-521-88315-6

22 Check the Viyou Inc. case study, which teaches how to integrate the environments/contexts into the ongoing business planning. This case is available at www.entrepreview.net, in the "Riskless Entrepreneurship" section.

2.6 Risk Matrix

As explained throughout this chapter, the existing deficiencies in the different business areas are the source of losses. These deficiencies are a direct consequence of the weaknesses (i.e., sources of risk) that exist in an organization that operates within a context that may or may not be convenient to achieve the expected results.

It would seem clear when analyzing problems that may affect a business through time, that is necessary to gather these five factors (i.e., sources of risk, deficiencies, events, areas, and contexts) to study them simultaneously. Such exercises would point to the use of graphic elements (Figure 2.9), capable of gathering all this information, so that the manager can analyze the chain of causes and effects referred to above.

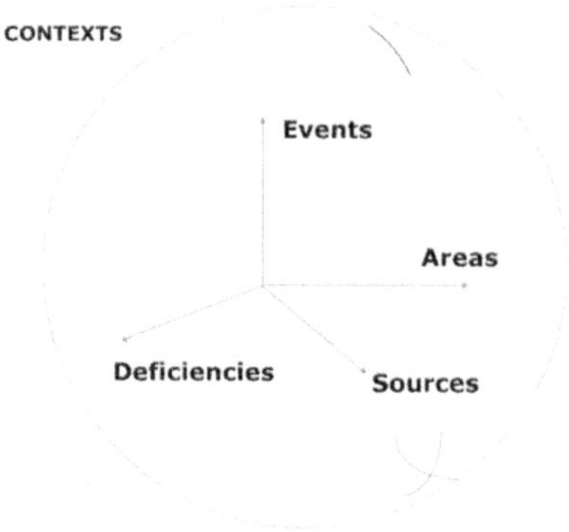

Figure 2.9
Graphic representation that suggests simultaneous management of events, areas, deficiencies, sources of risk and contexts

Unfortunately, the graphical representation capable of gathering such information looks difficult and impractical to design. That is why the desired correlation must be achieved with simpler formats. This means to partially group these variables, to have readings that explain, from different perspectives, the associated risks with the activities and analyzed processes.

Thus, tables or other graphic elements can relate variables of our interest. Here we do not talk about complicated alternative, since a simple list of probable events would already be a useful reference to those who examine a business.

However, there are also combinations of factors that can be constructed to explain, among others, a simple cause-and-effect relationship; or detect the existence of some pattern; or link variables of different nature or determine the relative importance of losses. In all these constructions, the idea will always be to organize information that helps us to understand the weak points of our business and their relative importance. Both variables make it easier to build work-maps that guarantee the efficient and hierarchical application of risk control.

An example is presented in Table 2.10. It summarizes the sources of risk identified in the different areas under analysis.

		Resources															
		Personnel			Organization			Assets			Information						
		Qualified	sufficient	Committed	Relevant	Updated	Difused	Available	Maintained	Secure	Effective	Efficient	Confidential	Integral	Available	Lawful	Trustworthy
Areas	Environment Link																
	Public opinión affairs				x												
	Administration & Control			x				x	x			x	x				
	Operation					x					x			x			
	Financial operations			x													
	Strategic planning			x				x				x					
	Trading													x			
	Compliance	x										x		x		x	

Table 2.10
Sources of risk of areas under review

Based on these matrices, we offer four recommendations that seem relevant to use this type of tool to support business analysis.

As suggested, this table is one of many that we can use to relate different variables. Additional examples are presented in Attachment D that illustrates different ways of correlating information and data that offer clues about real and potential problems.[23.]

Keep in mind that matrices can refer to information of any part of your business. By this, the information displayed may correspond to a

23 The case study ILUMITEC S.A. illustrates the best opportunity to consider matrices as work tools. This case is available at www.entrepreview.net, in the "Riskless Entrepreneurship" section.

specific unit (e.g., Matrix A), process (e.g., Matrix B), department or a complete business (e.g., Matrix C). As the analysis can be circumscribed to any part of the business, matrices can be constructed based on the viewpoint and detail of our interest.

Second, matrixes cannot only show events, deficiencies or risk sources. They are capable to present other information, such as amounts, severity, and hierarchies. For this, matrices can assume colors (e.g., Matrix D), letters (e.g., Matrix E), and numbers (e.g., Matrix F), or consider other formats (e.g., Matrix G) to order absolute and relative magnitudes that represent risks and their consequences.

Third, the classifications that organize areas, resources, and contexts, are simple guidelines that help understand the scope of these elements. Subsequently, the proposed families and subfamilies do not have to be used to identify them. It is good enough for entrepreneurs to define, in their way, the variables that help them design useful matrices.

Finally, matrices can contribute in gathering information on any aspect of the business, with the simple purpose of perfecting the analysis or complementing the planning of some particular element of the operation (See Matrix H). There are no limits on how we use information or how we mix data, assumptions, or projections. All the information required to examine risks may and should be included in the matrices to help explain all relevant aspects of the business.

We emphasize using matrices, for two fundamental reasons: On the one hand, they are the ideal tools to illustrate the vulnerability of a particular aspect of the business. Consider it as an effective way to present a well-summarized information to third parties.

On the other hand, building a matrix is an excellent exercise, since it forces entrepreneurs to think about the details of the business and to understand the dependence between the variables. As simple as a matrix may seem, the fact of identifying, summarizing and correlating much of the available information requires a considerable analytical effort.

We also recommend the incorporation of matrices into the tools that you will surely need to make an adequate assessment of your business. Be sure that over time you will be able to elaborate better analyses of your risks to foster bolder and more creative solutions.

Chapter 3. Risk Control

Risk Control helps us to decide if all
risks involved in performing our
new business are tolerable.

It is useful to introduce Risk Control, as the most important tasks of entrepreneurs. Controlling risks in the strategic phase means to use reliable sources of information when performing managerial analyses to get meaningful evidence and references to decide whether to make a business idea a reality.

Not identified omissions and deficiencies during this stage will surely become sources of risk. Not only because our understanding about the business and its contexts will be more limited. In addition, they expose us to starting the business operation without the resources that make it safer.

What is Risk Control?

Risk Control is not pure science, but a managerial discipline that demands skills and knowledge from different technical areas and sciences to approach, measure, and mitigate diverse sources of risks.

Likewise, running a business with unfinished planning will result in more wasted time and unforeseen costs, in a stage where resolving deficiencies could lead to important events.

For these reasons, we have included in this chapter a simplified explanation of risk control, where we discuss to the processes that make it possible. Subsequently, we indicate the risk control relevance in the business's evolution, to finally check the importance of adopting it from the same strategic phase.

Reflections on the difficulties of putting into practice a thorough risk control should be considered as a mandatory task, not as an option. This is the pivotal point of any planning exercise, as well as an important reference in defining the value of the business we are building.

3.1 How do we define Risk Control?

After clarifying the concept of "Risk," we can now define what "Risk Control" is. To set the term, we review definitions proposed in different international standards about this subject, that we summarize as follows:

"Risk control is a process designed in business planning, to make the personnel adopt a set of practices aimed at detecting, evaluating, and addressing the existing sources of risk that can affect business equity."

The above definition includes the term "process" since we are referring to a set of activities designed to identify, measure, evaluate, and act on the existing sources of risk. Such activities are part of a continuing work cycle that never stops because risks do not disappear, but they transform.

On the other hand, the definition shows that Risk Control is part of the business planning process from the very moment of devising the objectives and goals. Likewise, Risk Control will be included in the business budget when considering the investment and expenses required to perform the agreed-upon control policies.

Based on this approach, the origin of risk sources and their subsequent control are the set of decisions and strategies included in business planning. In other words, when we decide to maintain, to grow, or address new businesses or diversify the existing one, we are defining the type and magnitude of risk that we are going to face. Consequently, it is also our decision to access the resources that allow controlling the unavoidable "vulnerability conditions."

Risk Control Disciplines

Risk Control adopts modeling tools, statistical mathematics, internal controls, auditing and planning. Its personality rests on the way to identify, measure, and analyze events that demand corrective action.

Finally, this concept is part of the primary aim of protecting the business' equity, whose integrity and growth will depend on events of multiple nature and importance. As we will confirm throughout this book, it is not a coincidence that the concepts presented so far point at "business equity" as the highest priority.

3.2 The risk control process

Implementing Risk Control involves a process adaptable to any type, size, or degree of the business's development. In fact, the broad consensus on this control turned it into the standard that today governs this managerial discipline[24].

---

24 Among the most important standards worldwide, we have: Committee of Sponsoring Organizations of the Treadway Commission (COSO), www.coso.org/ ; ASNZ 4360 Australian and New Zealand Standard on risk Management (www.standards.govt.nz); COBIT Control Objectives for Information and Related Technologies https://www.isaca.org/ ISO 31000 - Risk management

Because of its reliability, many legal frameworks that regulate the operations of relevant economy sectors (e.g., Banks and Investment Firms) accept Risk Control as the basis for the supervision they exert[25].

In its very basic version, Risk Control presupposes a cyclical process that involves four essential steps, namely: Identification, Measurement, Analysis, and Actions. (See Figure 3.1)

Figure 3.1
Risk Control cycle[26]

"Identification," as its name suggests, includes the activities that identify past events in each area under scrutiny, as well as the analyzes that seek to predict potential events.

"Measurement" quantifies the potential impact that may occur over time, regardless of the cause, form, or dependency of the different events. These exercises quantify the real or potential impact of the weaknesses, which makes it possible to rank them and decide on which control to apply.

---

http://www.iso.org/iso/home/standards/iso31000.htm); A Risk Management Standard – IRM/Alarm/AIRMIC 2002 (https://www.theirm.org/

25 Because of its impact on the global stock markets, we should name the Dodd-Frank Act for the Wall Street Reform and Consumer Protection of 2010, as well as the Sarbanes-Oxley Act of 2002 also known as "Reform of the Law for businesses public accountants and investor protection "

26 There are adaptations of this cycle adopted by different control entities, as occurs with the European Food Safety Authority EFSA. https://efsa.gitlab.io/multimedia/riskassessment/index.htm

The "Analysis", apply both to those activities where events occurred, and those where never happened. Such foresight allows planning preventive solutions that avoid damage to the business.

Risk control should be...

- A continuous exercise that contributes to improving management.
- A source of risk census that should be considered in business planning.
- A review of effective use of resources.

The design of the measures that mitigate the sources of risk will be the basis for performing the "Actions". The latter is the execution of the agreed solutions to control the identified weaknesses.

There are actions to take, which are usually organized in diverse groups, among them: risks control, risk transfer, designing contingency plans, changing the risk form, or increasing the business capital.

The selection of these actions will be possible after prioritizing the sources of risk importance and identifying the weaknesses that justify them[27].

3.3 Why is Risk Control necessary?

At this point, the reader should understand the importance of Risk Control and its application in all kinds of business.

To confirm this idea, we may review the structure of large organizations to identify an entity that manages this control. Not only formally, when a high-level unit oversees this area. Organizations also invest substantial resources in training their employees to become part of a control network able to identify and manage the risks.

There are solid reasons that have forced this evolution to happen quickly[28]:

1. We must put into practice Risk Control to avoid, at least, catastrophic events. However, low-impact risk sources, which may exist in every area, can accumulate to the point of becoming important

---

27 Lam, James. Enterprise Risk Management: From Incentives to Controls. John Wiley and Sons 2014. ISBN-13: 978-1118413616

28 Enterprise Risk Management Initiative is an entity that investigates and promotes the subject of risks. You can read their reports about risk control and the challenges to implement it at https://erm.ncsu.edu/

losses. This translates into corporations becoming more proactive and aware of this phenomenon and demanding a more significant effort from their managers.

2. Risk control has become a formal discipline whose theoretical framework offers guidelines that supplement the corporations' strategic planning. This makes it impossible for companies to separately consider these two disciplines when planning and managing a business.

3. Regulators have focused on Risk Control. In the banking industry, for example, the Basel Committee[29] has openly promoted longstanding discussions with the world's leading financial institutions. One topic has been the method of quantifying the capital of financial institutions based on the level of risk involved in their operations. This and other initiative have promoted a legal frame widely adopted by global banking systems.

4. Today, there is a higher reliance on technology, which has changed the form and magnitude of events, as well as the cost of mitigating them. In short, top management recognizes that there is a more significant risk exposure[30]. It proposes a more organized work-plan to prevent the occurrence of events that may negatively impact a corporation's balance sheet.

Although incipient businesses cannot afford a specialized unit to manage Risk Control, its promoters cannot ignore this area for several reasons:

1. Risk also exists in young businesses causing more devastating effects due to the size of their capital and the lack of resources to implement controls.

2. The expected business profitability is a function of its inherent risks. If we don't deal with them integrally, the project valuation could be unrealistic. Such a situation, from the entrepreneur's point of view, could lead to the operation of the business without meeting the minimum conditions to exploit it profitably.

3. Incomplete planning or risk controls will mean delays and additional costs that will postpone the achievement of the original objectives.

---

29 The Basel Committee is the usual name by which the Basel Committee on Banking Supervision is known. It is a global organization that has joined banking supervision authorities since 1975, to strengthen the financial system soundness. Ver http://www.bis.org/

30 We recommend reading the firm Allianz report, "Allianz Risk Barometer", or the annual business risk report of Bank of America.

For new companies, this can mean the difference between surviving and shutting down.

Therefore, controlling risks does not vary among business, regardless of their activity, size, or complexity. Perhaps it depends more on the scope, capacity, and specialization of the entity that carries out such control, a condition that depends on the business's evolution.

¿? Vulnerability?

- Few people to work on many duties
- Lack of resources
- Weak planning
- No priorities definition
- No market experience

3.4 Business stages' risk control evolution

While "Risk" is latent throughout the life of a business, the means to plan and execute its control depends primarily on the size and evolution of that business. To illustrate this relationship, let us review the typical pattern of business evolution to understand how to exercise the Risk Control in every stage[31].

In general, a business that survives the changes and limitations of its beginning could achieve at least five stages of development, represented in Graph 3.2

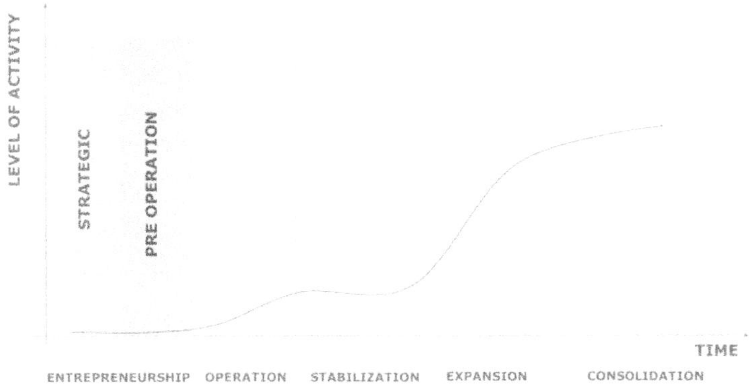

Graph 3.2
Typical business life's stages

31 Neil Petch "The Five Stages of Your Business Lifecycle: Which Phase Are You In?" Forbes Magazine, Feb 2016

At each stage, the business management faces different responsibilities because of the priorities that change over time. During this process, business development requires attention to a growing number of activities, and a higher number of internal and external agents (stakeholders). It demands extensive and more complex supervision, more efficient management, as well as compliance with a growing number of legal duties that increase the complexity of the business (See Table 3.3).

ENTREPRENEURSHIP		OPERATION	STABILIZATION	EXPANSION	CONSOLIDATION
STRATEGIC	PRE OPERATION				
• Idea formulation • Creation of the model or prototype of the product/service • Forecasting the operating budget/investment • Define a suitable business plan • Define the required funding • Contact available funding sources • Capital structure definition • Founding the company	• Adjustment of budget according to available funds • Constitution of the premise or local • Comply with basic formal duties • Acquisition of assets • Purchase of supplies, raw material, other • Recruitment of staff and outsourcings • Staff training • Projection of results	• Set up the customer network • Execution of the investment plan • Recruitment of staff and outsourcings • Staff training • Delegation of responsibilities • Ordinary operation • Accounting the operation results	• Consolidate the information and data system • Establish a management control • Productive process optimization • Professionalize the management team • Market consolidation • Protect headquarters and physical assets • Audit processes	• New business planning • Valuation of new projects • Activate funding sources • Growth of the organizational structure (verticalization) • Update productive processes • Changes in the capital structure	• Expand the concept of marketing and service • Consolidate the relationship with suppliers • Develop the business governance • Simplify the organizational structure • Optimize the market share • Highlight the institutional image

Table 3.3
Typical tasks of every business stages

Thus, the Strategic stage (i.e., Phase 1 of stage 1) is strongly biased toward the plan and budget designs. They depend on the collection and checking of the information fed from different sources (e.g., market), as well as the design of the operation and financing of the business. Therefore, it is important to design the most convenient capital structure to negotiate the funding conditions with sponsors, partners, and creditors.

Because of its analytical character, and the role that it plays in the planning of the business, risk control depends on the quality of the "strategic process" accomplished during this phase. It will not only endorse the decision-making process regarding the business feasibility, or the type of partnership that should endorse it, but will also help to understand those factors bound to the promotion of a more organized and safer operation.

Then we have the Pre-operation phase (i.e., phase 2 of stage 1). It includes activities like setting up the business' physical headquarter/facility, as well as the acquisition of goods, equipment, inventories, and other resources (including human resources) needed to start the operation. The terms investment, development, adjustment, testing, and induction are common at this phase.

The guidelines to control the risks depend mainly on the general manager. Not only because this person must guarantee compliance with technical, legal, and commercial conditions. The manager should also set basic rules regarding the safety of employees, equipment, and other resources.

Attention to the accounting and regulatory aspects is usually delegated to third parties so that the minimum administrative guidelines are met to fulfill legal duties (e.g., taxes, creditor, and partner duties).

Operational stage is next (i.e., stage 2), by formally beginning with the first sale of the product or service. Throughout this stage, the business increases the productive and commercial scales. It requires the participation of a supervisory team. Recruitment and delegation of specific functions, market penetration, as well as incorporating assets, are essential activities that make up this stage.

The administration is becoming more sophisticated since it is not only responsible for accounting routines but also for auditing, which by correlation means to be part of the risk control. In those instances, business should establish basic guidelines for asset control, on top of regular inventory auditing. It is uncommon to observe the implementation of risk control policies beyond the guidelines on industrial safety set by laws and regulations when applicable.

Stabilization (i.e., stage 3) is a process of consolidation of achievements. It is where management control and the development of suppliers and customers relationships come hand in hand with the management's professionalization.

In this stage, there is no significant increase in operations, but an increase in quality as a formula to maintain the market position. Consequently, all controls and policies aimed at safeguarding the benefits generated by the operation are an essential part of this stage. Here, auditors (internal or external) play an active role in controlling the risks of the organization.

Those businesses that aim at a larger productive scale will usually consider the expansion (growth) of their capacity (i.e., stage 4). It can happen either by expanding the same business or by acquiring other companies to guarantee production or sales.

Here, the critical issues are the search for financing, the synergies, the planning operations, and possibly changing the composition of the business' capital structure, which usually precedes the decision to grow.

At this stage of transformation, the planning unit sets the guidelines for business matters and risk control. It oversees the allocation of the resources necessary to operate. Of course, the other business units also strive to achieve the required resources to face the changes with the least possible risk. However, the planning team is the fundamental player controlling the risks since it defines strategies and allocates the resources for the entire organization.

Finally, it is possible to reach a new stabilization stage, after the company changes its operational scale (i.e., stage 5). Again, management tries to consolidate results, but now by simplifying structures and increasing business governance. It happens during this process that businesses make a more significant effort to improve their internal and external image by adjusting the controls of the critical business areas.

Once the adequate controls are implemented, it is possible to mitigate the risk sources, especially those that may cause a potential catastrophe capable of halting the operation, or events that may affect the quality of the products or services offered.

In this stage, it is necessary a risk specialist, given the business need for planning and implementing an ongoing control. Thus, identifying vulnerabilities, restructuring operations, and allocating resources are frequent tasks in a business that implements a risk controlling culture.

As mentioned before, this sequence is just illustrative, as it only tries to outline one of the many paths for the development of any business. The important thing to highlight, regarding Risk Control, is that no matter at what stage of business development we are, management can and must always make it part of its responsibilities.

3.5 Challenges in applying Risk Control

We have suggested that Risk Control is a discipline involved in the equity value protection. It is true since this exercise seeks to reduce non-budgeted losses as well as ensuring the continuity of the operations.

Assuming these controls entails a significant managerial effort, since gathering, analyzing, and distributing truthful information requires planning and long work hours. Not to mention what it means to establish an organizational culture that aligns the business's staff with the risk control process[32].

Adopting risk control

Measuring the real or potential effect of events helps to order sources of risk according to their importance. This work map is very difficult to ignore, even for those profit-oriented managers.

Despite difficulties, entrepreneurs must understand the advantages offered by the Risk Control if its implementation is gradual. As an illustration, we present arguments that help promote the staff involvement in such implementation:

1. Inviting the employees to adopt Risk Control as part of the day-to-day business routine, promotes the commitment to achieving excellence, and encourages a healthy competition for better management results. It is only possible to reach this condition if we explain the exact meaning and scope of the controls. This induction would seek to reduce the barriers usually created against the permanent revision that this control means.

2. The first steps must highlight the benefits of achieving a better performance. Then we must incorporate the staff into the control process, training them to identify the sources of risk in their work area.

3. The review of the processes and the activities undertaken by the organization is the control tool par excellence. It will help to discover the points that require auditing. But it also allows swapping not budgeted expenses (i.e., from unexpected events), with investments for resources for controlling every source of risk.

4. The control process also includes the creation and distribution of consistent information throughout the organization. It means that

---

32 Other challenges implementing risk control in organizations is arguing at; Negus Jim "10 Common ERM Challenges", Risk Management Magazine. March 2010. http://www.rmmagazine.com/2010/03/01/10-common-erm-challenges/

all employees should be well informed about the sources of risk across the business. Also, by knowing the ways to manage the sources of risk will increase their willingness to keep track of the agreed-upon controls.

The above process will meet its objectives if senior management understands that Risk Control helps to define a strategy in line with the business potential, since it takes into consideration the limitations created by the sources of risk.

Regarding this last point, consider that classic planning rarely contemplates the sources of risk when a business is defining its goals and plans. This old-style practice pays more attention to external contexts such as market behavior or special events that may affect operational capacity to reach desired qualities and costs.

In fact, increased competition, and the need to react safely to the rapid changes that occur in the markets, no longer allow omissions that, paradoxically, undermine the benefits of business planning.

Risk control should not be...

- An audit exercise that only identifies operational deficiencies
- A theorical approach managed only by managers
- A punitive mechanism against mismanagement

Therefore, the identification and communication of vulnerabilities are convenient for all. On the one hand, for the employees, who usually work without abundant resources to perform safe operations while they must fulfill goals that are often beyond their possibilities. On the other, it is convenient for the manager who's planning perspective only includes investments that "increase benefits," without considering the business operational weaknesses.

For all these reasons, Risk Control seems obvious. However, organizations are reluctant to take on this management option. One way to explain this resistance lies in the employees' unwillingness to openly discuss the problems they face, because it could be seen as a lack of capability for handling their duties[33].

33 The best term to describe this staff resistance is "fear". We suggest reading Michael and Elizabeth Umble "Overcoming resistance to change." Industrial Management, Jan 2014 publicado por iise.org en https://iise.org/Home/

This professional jealousy is especially significant in businesses where the organizational climate does not promote the importance of the employee. Under this circumstance, top management must have compelling arguments to establish a healthy control of the organization.

Keep in mind, when senior management defines goals, they are also establishing benchmarks to assess the staff's performance. To achieve realistic planning, it is necessary to identify each unit's weaknesses ahead of time. If it were not the case, goals would be challenging to attain. The mere need to reduce this potential gap between goals and results should reward employees when identifying the existing sources of risk in their daily tasks.

¿? Inducing Risk Control?

- Just training staff?
- Rewarding personnel when they identify and control a risk source?
- Penalizing those who omit the checking and control?

These and other difficulties inherent to implementing Risk Control could be minimized in new projects, as long as the founders are aware of incorporating these guidelines[34].

Hiring staff and forming an efficient team should include training in Risk Control, which leads to the establishment of rules for assessing the staff's performance. Doing it from the inception stages reduces the likelihood of facing resistance. It is an opportunity that the entrepreneur should take advantage of. However, we must know the order and discipline required when managing a company without deviating from this approach of doing business.

34 A useful reading about Risk Control implementation can be found on the page of ISO 31,000 standard at, https://www.isotools.org/

Chapter 4. The startup decision

At the very moment we decide to start up a business, we are defining the level of risk that we are willing to accept.

The flash of a "great idea" is usually a remarkable moment in the life of an entrepreneur. The conviction that the stars alignment has created a business opportunity takes the imagination on a journey through different scenarios projected with incredible details.

This initial euphoria dissipates once we realize that starting a business requires attention to a barrage of issues that continuously appear on to-do lists: meetings with potential vendors, the pre-selection of developers, and endless online research. This business phase is very dynamic, with elevated levels of uncertainty and anxiety.

With no pause but in hurry

Many entrepreneurs surpass their incipient plan by acquiring resources, services, or starting agreements without determining the project viability.

Aware of chaos during this early stage, we have consulted entrepreneurs who have endured these times. Through informal interviews, we could identify the above patterns, that helped us to establish two exercises that make it easier to reach rational decisions. The first task identifies the reasons that business founders wish to begin the project, while the second one identifies and evaluates potential success factors.

While these two exercises relate to personal issues, they have a lot to do with designing the work plan, since they help to define the elements that affect the decision to starting a project. Here, we mainly refer to the levels of risk and the business priorities.

We dedicate the first part of this chapter to explain these two concepts. Not only to understand their scope but also to establish a reasonable way to keep them top of mind while deciding on the new business.

In the second part, we review ineffective practices used by entrepreneurs when they manage their projects. These include pre-established ways of doing things, prejudices, and traditional rules of thumb that often limit the possibility of promoting a successful business.

In this chapter, there are no mathematical approaches, management theories, or complex exercises. Instead, there is a compendium of experiences from entrepreneurs with a wide range of results. These findings will undoubtedly save time and headaches during your start up. Therefore, we suggest carefully reading this experiences collection.

4.1 Reasons to launch a new business

As previously mentioned, starting a business is not just about making money. Actually, there are hundreds of reasons that make these initiatives a little more appealing.

Therefore, we have completed a census that shines a light on this topic. To analyze the results, we should remember that the reason someone undertakes a project justifies the work to do and the risk level to take.

At first sight, there are as many motives to start a business as there are entrepreneurs. However, it is possible to categorize the reasons into three groups (Figure 4.1)[35]

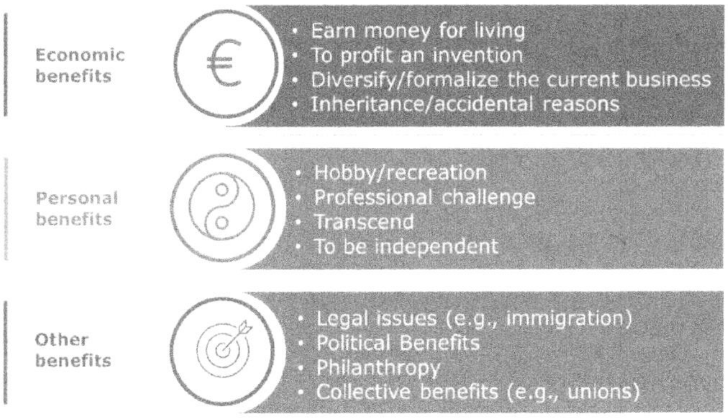

Figure 4.1
Reasons to undertake a new business (families)

The displayed distribution depends on the benefit. It is logic since every business must compensate its founders, either for economic or non-economic benefits. The experience shows that non-economic reasons complement most of the time the goal of making a profit.

These mixes of reasons complicate the one-founder initiatives, because egos, fears or commitments. Even more, these circumstances also condition associations, since agreeing with others on how to run and what to expect from a business can be a demanding exercise.

35 "50 Reasons to Start Your Own Business". Entrepreneur magazine, Feb 2015 https://www.entrepreneur.com/starting-a-business/50-reasons-to-start-your-own-business/243145

The classic example we present here is a project started by two entrepreneurs with different income levels. One already has a comfortable lifestyle not dependent on the project's success, while the other partner needs this business to cover his standard of living.

Under these circumstances, there are business aspects where they do not share the same views, such as profit distribution versus reinvesting to grow the business, only because money means something different to each one.

¿? Successful Entrepreneurship ?

Is a successful enterprise dependent on a singular market opportunity, on how we manage the project or the lucky of developing a best-seller?

We do not imply that such differences between partners would automatically lead to disagreements. However, there must be a strategy to address different interests and priorities that would not hinder the progress of the business.

4.2 Elements of Success

In addition, starting a company must be justifiable to the entrepreneurs by bringing evidence about its possibilities of achieving acceptable results.

In business, there are circumstances, coincidences, and even accidents that create excellent opportunities for investment. However, a cautious entrepreneur knows things may not be what they appear, and business requires more than a fortunate history to be profitable.

In this context, a smart entrepreneur must complete unemotional analyses by identifying the pros and cons, and by considering the real possibility that a business could fail as others have.

Business risk

People usually explain the business risk in term of the relative size investment to the investor wealth, the business legal exposure or the guarantees for creditors. However, this risk indeed depends on our ability to carry the business out with the available resources in the existing contexts.

Through this exercise, we can discover the actual success factors, thus taking advantage of a potential business opportunity. Among the answers that we must find, there is one related to discovering the "Elements of Success" that could favor the project we have in mind. Such an analysis involves identifying and weighing elements, based on their importance (See Figure 4.2) [36]

Figure 4.2
Elements of success (Families)

Again, what is relevant here is not the families themselves, but the different situations illustrated through each success element. In real life, the advantages that could portend excellent results are more.

Regarding the advantages, an entrepreneur should not assume the rule to promote only businesses that depend on an exceptional situation.

Indeed, the possession of a singular asset (e.g., land with a premium location), the access to favorable financing conditions (e.g., subsidized credit) or the exclusive right to exploit an asset (e.g., patents), can be excellent reasons to carry out a business. However, these advantages will not be enough to achieve the desired success if an entrepreneur does not have the resources and the ability to leverage them.

Keep in mind that managing a business has more to do with our point of view than with realistic truths. This increases the risk of overvaluing our abilities, as well as erroneously estimating the value added by elements of success that seem to favor us[37].

---

36 This perspective differs from most authors when defining success's key factors. Michael Damian proposes an existentialist point of view "3 Keys to Entrepreneurial Success". Entrepreneur Magazine April 2019. https://www.entrepreneur.com/article/332662
A more structured study is published by Reid, G.C. and Smith, J.A.. (2000)." What makes a new business start-up Successful?" Small Business Economics, 14, 165-182. https://www.researchgate.net/publication/5158015_What_Makes_a_New_Business_Start-Up_Successful
37 Business success is distorted by myths that affect our expectations as business founders. Please read Mohammed, Shah. "Survivorship Bias, Entrepreneurship and The Myth Of Becoming Successful" https://shahmm.medium.com/survivorship-bias-entrepreneurship-and-the-myth-of-becoming-successful-1d60c1606908

The only recipe to counteract these illusions is still to carry out a complete and objective planning.

4.3 Critical factors

It is useful to recognize the entrepreneur's abilities for achieving the best possible results. However, it is also important to denote the "critical factors" that could guide a new business towards failure.

To illustrate this, Table 4.3 presents a list of factors that usually require more attention during the planning stage of every business. Although many of those factors seem obvious, they are the most likely to affect the performance of these types of projects.

COFFEE FARM		RESTAURANTS	
Critical Factors	Events/deficiencies	Critical Factors	Events/deficiencies
Climate and land	Harvest loss per pest	Climate and land characteristic	Theft from staff
Market price	Coffee plants aging	Market price	Noncompliance with duties
Fungi/plague control	Climate. Rain out of time	Fungi/plague control	Food contamination
Experience/tech knowledge	Bad grain collection	Experience/technical knowledge	High staff turnover
PHYSICAL REHAB CENTER		**GAS STATION**	
Critical Factors	Events/deficiencies	Critical Factors	Events/deficiencies
Staff technical expertise	Congestion/poor attention	Location, location, location	Accidents with gas pumps
Equipment's availability	Not reach break-even point	Safety standards application	Fines for breaches
Location	Wrong patients' treatment	Store/other services	Lack of safety
Insurance companies	Accounts receivable managing	Supplier/inventory control	Lack of inventory
LADY'S FASHION BOUTIQUE		**AUTO REPAIR**	
Critical Factors	Events/deficiencies	Critical Factors	Events/deficiencies
Positioning in the right niche	Inventory's obsolescence	Workshop capacity/quality	Delays or repairs failed
Inventory management	Lack of niche access	Accounts Receivable	Staff turnover
Define price/quality ratio	Noncompliance with duties	Insurance companies	Accounts receivable increase
Location	Non updated offer	Parts/Spare Parts Suppliers	Damage/loss tools/equipment

Table 4.3
Critical factors for different businesses.
Potential events from poor factors control

Beyond these factors, there are two that exist in all businesses that demand a more thorough planning: the work team and the partnership.

If you start up with an efficient team and you identify the right partners, you are halfway to success with your new business. This statement does not downplay other critical factors. However, the impact of the human resource is so crucial for a business to succeed that we place it first on the list.

To better explain this point of view, in the next two sections we expose considerations regarding the ability to gather a good team. Keep an eye of this information because it may be crucial for your entrepreneurship.

a. Work Team selection

We start with the fundamental argument that people are the most valuable resource[38]. Every business requires funding, equipment, contacts, and facility to settle down the operation. However, not having the right team will create challenges for new enterprises to start operations and achieve sustained growth.

We are not alluding to any work team. We are referring to one with the required conditions to achieve the business objectives. Among these attributes, we should consider preparation, experience, seriousness, moral fiber, and commitment (Figure 4.4).

Figure 4.4
Staff best qualities

Few businesses have been blessed with a team that gathers all these attributes. Nevertheless, we should always strive to search for candidates with the qualities that can help us succeed in a challenging and uncertain journey. To form a high-quality team, the entrepreneur needs to carry out a set of processes (Figure 4.5).

38 Remember that your employees will be, like it or not, your "first partners" since you are inevitably trusting them with your business results.

The first and most important one is the selection of candidates. To find qualified people, we need to design the application and selection phases carefully. The idea is not only to increase the number of candidates for each position, but also to access the variety of profiles that the labor market can offer.

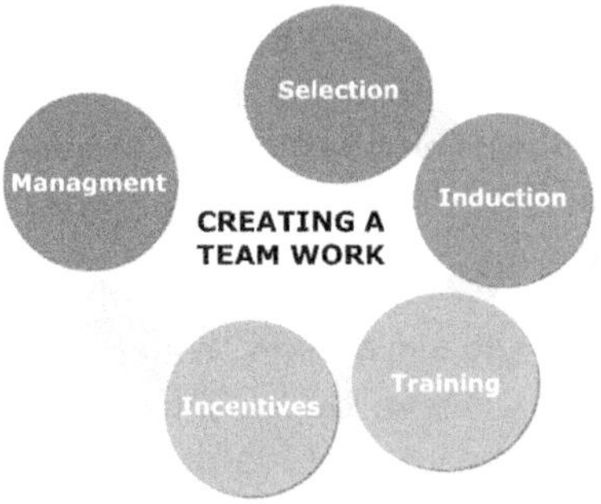

Figure 4.5
Processes to create a teamwork

The onboarding and training of new employees include a set of exercises, instructions, and information sharing. The idea is to make clear our expectations about the results they must achieve. Even when the employees possess the experience and initiative to perform duties, it is also desirable to familiarize them to the business specifics and resources for them to be more productive.

Aside from improving employee work productivity, ongoing training will allow them to better understand the operation, harness their potential and make them gain confidence, which leads to their commitment to the business objectives. The latter factor is crucial to avoid losing employees when a company does not promise significant professional growth because of its size or structure. This loss results in a higher turnover rate for wholly or partially trained employees and it significantly reduces the likelihood of success of the new business[39].

39 Ken Moon, Prashant Loyalka, Patrick Bergemann , Joshua Cohen "The Hidden Cost of Worker Turnover: Attributing Product Reliability to the Turnover of Factory Workers" Management Science, Mar 14, 2022, https://doi.org/10.1287/mnsc.2022.4311

¿? Incentives

Do these incentives apply to stimulate only the technical, administrative, and managerial employee? Or they can also reward workers?

Next, we have the incentives which include the salary, bonuses, and other benefits. To compensate employees comprehensively, the incentives should be competitive, adjusted to each employee's profile, and flexible to reward the achievement of their set goals.

Even though the incentives may match the market standards, they do not guarantee the employee's motivation and loyalty to continue in the company. The departure of an outstanding employee usually creates chaos in the business. To avoid this setback, entrepreneurs need to be highly creative in protecting human capital, by considering incentives such as conditional bonuses, or shareholding for key employees[40].

Finally, Management includes the control, coordination, and monitoring of the work team.

There are management styles related to various sensitive business affairs, like the transparency in handling information, the employee involvement in the planning process, as well as the definition of incentives and bonuses. There are no universal guidelines for managing factors like these. The management style depends on the character and experience of the business founder. However, openness and confidence and the sense of gratitude and recognition are well received by employees, since they help create an efficient, stable, and highly motivated team.

Human resources

The human is the most critical resource since the existing and potential sources of risk depend, ultimately, on our staff's professional and personal weaknesses.

We recommend entrepreneurs take time to assess this crucial aspect, by deciding on what management style to adopt, and considering the employees' level and the nature of their work. Keep always in mind that people are an essential resource for any startup, so it will reward the time and effort to plan its management.

---

40 Melissa Van Dyke, titulado "Motivating today´s workforce: The Future on Incentives and Recognition Program Design". http://theirf.org/research/motivating-todays-workforce-the-future-of-incentive-program-design/179/

b. Creating the partnership

As previously stated, entrepreneurs must face a crucial decision on how to move forward and build their business by evaluating, for example, the advantages and disadvantages of self-financing or accessing other financial sources (i.e., partnership or debt)[41].

The capital structure design is a critical element that demands a dispassionate planning from the project's very early stages to safeguard the business continuity.

Entrepreneurs need to follow a procedure to set a capital structure by considering four primary variables:

1. Planned business activity
2. Amount of any foreseen investment
3. Entrepreneurs' contributions.
4. Targeted equity participation, consistent with the capital structure

From these variables, it is possible to define a workplan to determine the available financial resources. Once we establish these resources, we should identify their pros and cons, as well as design a strategy to enhance the attractiveness of our project[42].

When it comes to choosing the source of funding, we need to comply with certain requirements, such as presenting a business plan, preparing contracts, defining the statutes or company's bylaws, and providing any other information needed to start the business[43].

Once those basic requirements are met, entrepreneurs must then determine whether to start the project with or without the association with third parties based on the source of financing. Remember that self-financing would always be an entrepreneur's first choice, given the speed

---

41 Please read the Stanford University report on the financing of businesses promoted by Latinos in the United States. https://www.gsb.stanford.edu/faculty-research/publications/latino-owned-businesses-shining-light-national-trends

42 The case study "Negotiating the CoCoe's brand" addresses the partnerships' definition. This case is available at www.entrepreview.net, in the section "Riskless Entrepreneurship".

43 Levin, Marisa. "6 Steps to Creating a Partnership That Drives Strong Business Growth", Inc.com, Jan 2018 https://www.inc.com/marissa-levin/6-steps-to-creating-a-partnership-that-drives-strong-business-growth.html

and simplicity in disbursing the funds. However, if there is risk aversion or any limitation to providing the required funds, we must then investigate alternative sources, like partnering with investors, a creditor agreement, or a combination of both.

If the decision is to partner with investors, we should establish a criterion to evaluate the candidates. At the very least, it is necessary to consider factors such as their contribution (i.e., money, other resources) their capacity to accomplish the work to be done, their knowledge and business experience, as well as their networks and contacts. Additionally, there are personal issues to consider, such as commitments, friendships, kinships, mutual trust, or merely their prestige.

The reason you choose will always be valid. Remember two important things: first, many of the resources we receive from a partnership can also be obtained from other sources. (Table 4.6) Second, your partner will share with you as much of the cost as the benefits of your project. In whatever sense, the concept of "equity" has absolute priority.

POSSIBLE CONTRIBUTIONS FROM POTENTIAL PARTNERS	ALTERNATIVE PROVIDER
Money	Banks, business, family funds
Work/Management Capacity	Employees
Headquarters	Real-estate market
Contacts and network	Friends, family, colleagues
Equipment, tools	Suppliers
Legal/labor counseling	Firms specializing in each field
Problems and discussions	Conjugal partner

Table 4.6
Alternative sources to the partner contributions

We must ponder when deciding the business capital structure, since every association has both costs and benefits. As the number of partners grows, it will be harder to reach a consensus. Therefore, when creating a partnership, the founder must clarify if it is crucial to have one or more partners.

Even though it may seem like it, we do not have an animosity towards partnerships. When an association is adequately formed, there is no better way to develop a business. However, entrepreneurs must vet the partners they have in mind to increase the probability of the project's success[44]. If in doubt, check and adjust the "invitation list" as many times as you see fit[45].

Suppose that you, as an entrepreneur, invite one or more acquaintances to take part in the project as partners. The questions that you should answer include:

1. How to determine the value of each partner's contributions? Will you only take monetary contributions into account?

2. What effort and time can the partners provide to the business? Will you consider their performance as a part of the contributions?

3. Once you have determined the value of a contribution, what type of criteria will you adopt to offer an attractive participation, without unfairly reducing yours?

Do not undermine the importance of this exercise. You, as a promoter, must create very solid arguments to sell your project. But you must also offer a fair share for contributions you expect to receive from each partner.

Finding this balance point complicates the foundation of companies but attending formally to this process is imperative. Do not skimp on any resources, time, or effort to complete this analysis that will eventually be rewarded with stability and synergy[46].

Risky partnerships

Uncertainty is a key factor when we are partnering. The less reliability the project offers, the greater the risk premium will request the capital contribution agreed upon. This premium might be a larger shareholding that guarantees control or a higher rate of return, which means a lower project implicit value.

Take your time when deciding. Review the pros and cons. Keep in mind that you can outline the formal equity allocation during the entrepreneurship process, once you have facts, studies, or evidence of your project's success. The Devil is in the details and by hastily defining shareholding without evaluating each partner's contribution means that one

44 Harroch, Richard, "20 Things All Entrepreneurs Should Know About Angel Investors FEB 5", 2015, Forbes Magazine https://www.allbusiness.com/angel-investing-20-things-entrepreneurs-should-know-20552-1.html

45 Check this topic reading the case study " Automotive Service Center " available at www.entre-preview.net, in the section "Riskless Entrepreneurship".

46 This equity distribution exercise is always "zero sum". von Neumann, J.; Morgenstern, O. (1944). Theory of Games and Economic Behavior. Princeton University Press New Jersey

of you will lose money. This equity allocation exercise is a zero-sum game.

When meeting with all potential associates, invite them to openly participate. Meanwhile, your team will define roles, and build your business according to your vision. If possible, delay the decision to distribute the equity until each associate understands the balance between costs and benefits of any assumed commitment. Once you have defined the project's direction, quantifying the contributions' value will be a fair and easier exercise.

4.4 Typical oversights when starting up

This is a short selection of the "habits" that many entrepreneurs adopt when starting their businesses, without realizing the implicit sources of risk they create.

We vehemently discourage the use of "shortcuts" or "common sense rules" that are usually adopted and downplaying the importance of undertaking a complete entrepreneurship exercise[47].

Those are things that should not happen in your company despite the opinion of others who say they have previously applied them with positive results.

a. Start from the beginning. "Sales"

Although "the idea" is the spark that triggers a new business, "sales" is the "verb" of your enterprise. There is no clever idea if we cannot sell it. For doing it, you must first go to the market and find out who has the need or the desire to purchase/use the product/service you plan to offer[48].

---

47 Rahman Almutaz "Common mistakes Entrepreneurs make and How to avoid them" Forbes, Feb 2021. https://www.forbes.com/sites/forbesbusinesscouncil/2021/02/12/common-mistakes-entrepreneurs-make-and-how-to-avoid-them/?sh=2a6d2a913d67

48 If you buy this introduction, then you will not be interested anymore in those projects that omit the description of the potential client who has the pleasure/need to consume/use the product/service.

Whether it is a product or service, a good offer is always well-positioned in a market eager to acquire it under conditions where the seller can make a profit.

When referring to a well-positioned product/service, we are not talking about personal points of view. We refer to a comprehensive concept, which is very well explained by traditional marketing[49].

We point it out in this way, since the entrepreneurs' perceived peculiarity of their product/service will be the one factor that will push them to start a business, only if it is desired by potential clients or consumers.

To find these consumers, we must create a profile of those that theoretically have the need or desire to acquire our product/service. Then, we must find a group that fits our profile so we can confirm their tastes and preferences regarding our offer.

If possible, we should have a sample or prototype on hand for a more realistic assessment. But even in the absence of a prototype, it is always possible to consult with colleagues, relatives, friends, and friends of friends, regarding our product/service idea.

Depending on the results of those queries, it will be possible to have a clearer idea of who our potential client is. But before designing a marketing plan and inviting them to try our product/service, we must first establish the concept of the product/service, as well as the means to present it and evaluate it.

Once you have decided on the means of consultation (e.g., surveys, meetings), find as many potential clients as you can[50]. Go and find them, in the streets, venues, public squares or in an office. Practice your pitch. Become their friend. Discuss your idea and even ask them for advice. Show them your prototype and ask for help to identify flaws you can improve.

¿? Planning references

If you deal with a pioneering project in your location, what references are useful to figure out its future performing? Similar business in other locations? Other business in the same location? Or not considering other business at all?

49 Kotler Philip, Armstrong Gary, "Marketing fundamentals", Pearson (2003 or newer editions)
50 Often, some market players end up being the best sources of information. We refer to suppliers, entrepreneurs, and the competitors themselves.

Talk to them about prices and costs. Let them be your counselors for a moment. Take their opinion seriously. It does not matter if they are a housewife or an engineer. Listen to them as if they were the most renowned marketing consultants.

If you have the perseverance and the fortune to carry out a survey like this one, you must expect great surprises. But more importantly, you will have a complete guide to the qualities and flaws of your idea.

You will know first-hand how you can offer your product/service, what things to improve and what features to exploit. You can have specific data on how to consume/use it and you can even have a good reference to fix the price/rate that your customers would pay.

With this roadmap, you will ratify whether (or not) you have a product/service with a real demand. Then you will decide whether it is worth continuing your entrepreneurship process.

b. No rule of three in business

It is false that the results got from projects like ours will be necessarily the one we are going to achieve. This is equivalent to thinking that, if many could open a bakery, we can also sell bread.

¿? Successful business

Being successful in any type of business increase the chances of success in other businesses? Or in other words. Is success a condition that, after being achieved, it will never be lost?

Unfortunately, this reasoning is wrong, even if we have more success probabilities than our predecessors. Other businesses results are not applicable to our project. Therefore, do not let your guard down by trusting that "providence" will compensate for our omissions.

This recommendation is important, even for those who have been successful in promoting other businesses. Being overconfident and skipping the evaluation and planning routine before deciding on your investment is common in these cases.

This assertion does not undermine the "gut feeling" that businesspeople develop for the opportunities or inconveniences of each business. But playing "King Midas" by assuming unique abilities to predict the fate of our project, may be quite excessive.

Certainly, the strategy of imitating successful people is widespread and happens in sectors as sophisticated as the capital markets[51].

Even for ordinary investors who decide to buy securities, or undertake a business, their previous experiences always play a role in that decision. However, past positive results are not good enough reference for evading the planning that must precede a sound business decision[52]

c. Projects evolve

Something that usually bothers many entrepreneurs is the change that the original project undergoes during its planning and implementation.

We are not only talking about the change in size, complexity, or the business model. Projects can be transformed in ways that can even change their mission and objectives. There are three fundamental reasons for these metamorphoses to occur: On the one hand, founders rarely have the information and experience to foresee what their project entails.

These deficiencies are quite common in innovative businesses. But also, in the more traditional ones, whose founders were unaware of basic and not so basic business topics (e.g., legal barriers).

Long and complex projects

If you are launching an ambitious project, think about developing it in parts. Establish stages according to a realistic schedule is a smart way to eat the whole pie (i.e., piece by piece)

On the other hand, it happens that the pre-existing conditions to develop the project can change and even disappear.

Here we refer, for instance, to the money that was supposed to be available, to the defection of a strategic partner, or the impossibility of buying an asset under some agreed-upon specifications. Changing some premises can transform a project until it becomes unfeasible under the originally assumed conditions.

---

51 Following up on successful investors is a subject for some agencies. Here, the basic assumption is that these investors know something that the rest of the market does not know when they invest or cash out.

52 You can read other points to consider when evaluating a business idea at "For Dummies" articles "10 Ways to Evaluate a New Business Idea". https://www.dummies.com/business/start-a-business/business-plans/10-ways-to-evaluate-a-new-business-idea/

Finally, the project may present inconsistencies or may require an extraordinary simultaneity of conditions. These mismatches reduce the chances of achieving the expected goals, and this often forces us to change our business perspective.

Accepting that "changes" are the norm, entrepreneurs must be willing to pursue a consistent planning exercise.

Convenient partnerships

The entrepreneur's commitment is not only related to the invested resources. It is also based on the commitment to partners, employees, suppliers, and customers.

Indeed, the changes may occur up to a certain limit in order to continue with the same project, which may be a critical condition for certain business initiatives[53]. However, in most cases, the final version of the business will only have to respond to our preferences, interests, and abilities.

In fact, when you complete your planning process, we invite you to cold analyze the result. You will identify critical elements that have undergone important changes regarding the original business idea. It usually happens as a product of establishing a plan more related to the existing contexts and resources than your original premises.

So don't be alarmed by changes in your strategic exercise. Trying different formulas to create a competitive version of your idea is desirable, which, by definition, could lead you to proceed with a business different from the one you originally envisioned.

d. Do not neglect the value concept

The value is the profitability that an investment could offer and, hence, is the most important reference when making a business decision.

Here, we are not only referring to the simple mathematical exercise of discounting "probable cash flows" to get their current value. Value is a comprehensive concept that involves measuring convenience, but also the possibility of adopting strategies to exploit the business in the environments that may affect its performance.

This does not mean choosing operational and financial variables that maximize value. Rather, it means proposing logical strategies based on

53 We refer to, for example, projects with limited financing plans, or operations that must fulfill very strict technical conditions.

our possibilities to make them come true. Once the plans have been identified, they must be converted into variables, limits, or conditions that will be considered in the cash flow projection.

If this exercise is well-performed, the value should be the pivot of the business plan. This means that we can rate any plan (e.g., operations, sales, or financing) suitability/reliability based on their aggregated value.

Since this perspective is not popular, it is difficult to find business proposals generated under rigorous evaluations. Partly for the difficulty of creating models, getting the information, and correctly applying the cash flow discount method. But, in addition, translating scenarios into numerical variables is a demanding exercise that requires experience in evaluating businesses.

Although this subject demands a more detailed explanation[54], for now, we invite entrepreneurs to face this exercise rigorously. So, take your time, seek expert help, and always question your results.

Remember that you are the first one to convince yourself of your own projections. This involves understanding the cause-effect relationship between the way you manage your business and the expected profitability from it. And the only function that makes this connection is value.

e. To not start is an option

As stated, entrepreneurship is an important life initiative that forces us to devote a lot of energy to turning an idea into a real business.

Such is the committed effort that the project becomes another family member. It eats, bathes and sleeps with us, even invading the space of family and friends. Losing objectivity about its feasibility is very easy, especially when entrepreneurs are not rigorous enough to evaluate, plan and execute their ideas.

In such circumstances, it is common for some disarray to occur when entrepreneurs assemble the business (e.g., purchasing resources, hiring.) before finishing the assessment and planning exercises.

---

54 Najul, Miguel, "Evaluación de proyectos". IESA editions 2010, Caracas Venezuela

This mainly happens because we are overconfident that we are developing a profitable business. This sentiment is so powerful that we will never consider the option to abandon it, even with evidence that the business is not profitable[55].

Good and better deals

Accepting good business is a desirable decision if there are conditions to do so. Rejecting bad business is an even better decision, although it is radical for most.

In these extreme situations, some prefer to "fix the problems" that may arise along the entrepreneurship process before considering canceling the project. They do not realize their misstep when they proceed with a project with little chances of success, wasting time, effort, and resources that they could invest in another business with better possibilities.

Even if it sounds repetitive, keep in mind that the antidote to avoid these "failed exercises" is to complete an orderly entrepreneurship process. With this, let us remind you that, analyzes regarding the potential of the project must precede the decision to undertake it.

Inverting the order or omitting steps, and continuous oversights, will lead to devoting efforts to an unclear business. Don't be afraid to face the decision to abandon your project. If it doesn't suit you, just don't do it. Abandoning it may be your best business decision ever.

55 Similar situation is treated at "GarageLock" case study, available at www.entrepreview.net, in the section "Riskless Entrepreneurship".

Chapter 5.
The Entrepreneurship's stage

We must understand the phase in which everything begins. A challenging moment when we design a viable strategy to convince others and ourselves to take the risk of investing.

As explained, the life of a business can be divided into stages, the first of which corresponds to entrepreneurship.

Likewise, this latter stage can be divided into two phases: Strategic and Pre-Operational. Such differentiation does not pretend to complicate the analysis by adopting an excessive and useless classification. It serves as a guide to accomplish in an orderly manner the tasks that precede our business operation.

Hence, the Strategic phase encompasses the previous study and evaluation that precedes the decision on whether launch the business. While in the Pre-Operational phase, we get the resources and build the company that will operate according to our plan.

This arrangement, whose simplest form is presented in Figure 5.1, is based on three milestones that start and finish each phase. (i.e., Idea, Build the business and First sales).

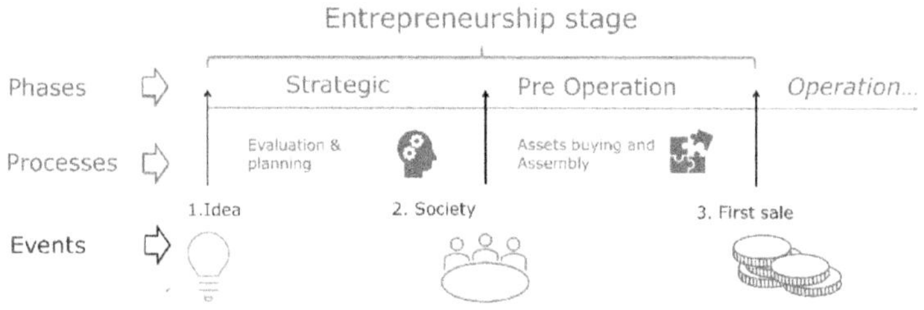

Figure 5.1
Entrepreneurship stage milestones

To establish the risk reduction as the ultimate reason for this classification, we devote this chapter to explaining what these stages comprise [56].

5.1 The Strategic Phase

Let's focus our attention on the first phase, that we have called "Strategic". This phase involves a set of analyses, consultations, studies,

56 The most detrimental condition for any entrepreneurship is ignoring what to do and/or why to do it. To avoid additional time and cost executing your planning exercise, we suggest carefully reading this chapter to take home a complete and safe work plan.

presentations, and negotiations that turn a simple idea into a startup with the resources to set up the planned business.

To achieve this conversion, during this phase we must accomplish five specific objectives (Figure 5.2): determine the technical/legal feasibility; establish the operating model; plan the market positioning; determine the business' financial feasibility and get the financing[57].

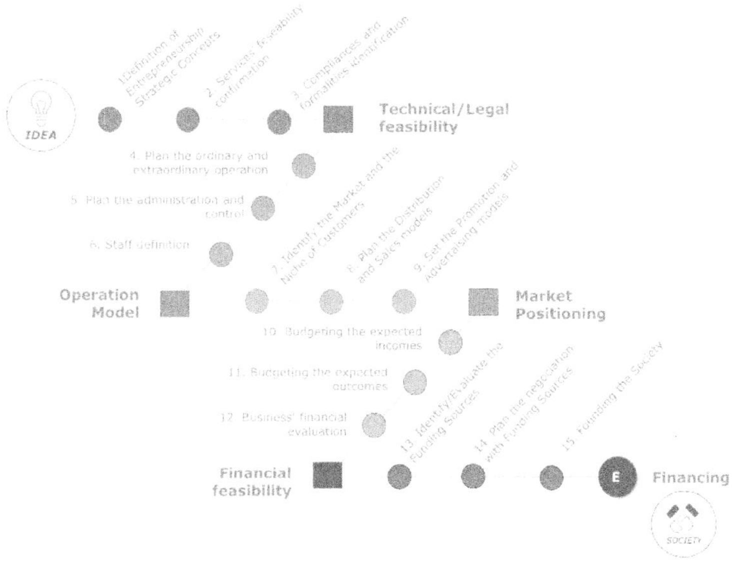

Figure 5.2
Strategic phase's objectives and processes
Case: Service business

To achieve these objectives, we must carry out at least fifteen different processes. These include all the actions required for gathering data and references needed to reach a business decision.

This way of planning a business has several attributes. It is effective, since it proposes the processes required to achieve the mentioned objectives. It is safe because the processes involve handling the new busi-

57 The way to organize the entrepreneurship stage may adopt different versions. For example, the agency "Small Business Administration, SBA", suggests the following: https://www.sba.gov/business-guide/10-steps-start-your-business

ness sources of risk. It is orderly since it groups the processes into topics. And it is comprehensive because it organizes the entire phase from a general to a specific perspective.

Keeping this last attribute in mind, notice that these processes have been identified generically. Executing them without additional specifications may prevent getting the required information.

To compensate for this lack of precision, we have defined a set of activities that include the consultations, studies, calculations, and projections that fulfill each process (See Attachment A tables) [58].

i! Activities to accomplish

The entrepreneurship exercise is long and demanding. To complete the strategic phase, Entrepreview® suggests 75 different activities. Each one demands abundant information to be consistent with the rest of the planning.

Though each activity may contemplate a set of more specific tasks and procedures, the work agenda defined in terms of activities is practical enough to carry out a complete planning exercise.

To understand how to achieve every objective, we explain the content and order of the processes that comprise them. The execution of the corresponding activities does not alter relations explained, but it guarantees a more complete form of planning.

a. From an initial idea to determining the project viability

To shape the business idea, entrepreneurs must collect an important volume of information.

Operations standard, production capacity and sales volumes are examples of the long list of elements to check. Not only understanding cost and efficiencies but considering how others have developed similar ideas by managing such variables. Notwithstanding that, these first reviews may not follow a specific order, it is necessary to consider all requirements (e.g., financial, technical) to make the product or service available.

Additionally, we must identify potential customers who want or need to consume/use it. Thus, entrepreneurs must get the inputs/components,

58 Readers must review this appendix to adopt this reliable work guide. Such a detail is offered by the ENTREPREVIEW platform. It offers a list of guides adjusted to the type of business you are dealing with.

recipes, and processes to elaborate the product, or identify the resources, skills, or technical instructions needed to develop the service.

It is convenient to create samples, design beta versions, or sketch the facilities in which to provide the service. These exercises organize the planning and will facilitate the introduction of the product/services to others who will surely identify its virtues and flaws.

Examples of a prototype:

Prepare a cake (Cake Manufacturer); Screens and reports layout (New App); Create decorative sketches (Decorative services). Draw the product when it's not possible to create a sample.

Once we corroborate that barriers to offering/providing the product/service are manageable, we must then identify the tasks to set up the business. We do not talk about a simple task list. Here, we refer to schedules and budgets, very useful when dealing with complex or long projects.

To effectively planning the business setup, entrepreneurs must consider all operating details to identify the resources that make it possible. This exercise is indispensable to get a preliminary investment and budgeting figures.

Gathering all these references will not be used to examine the business feasibility, but it will serve as an exercise that will allow us to understand the business scale, as well as the amount to finance.

Sources of risks

Litigations in the business world are increasing. In 2005, the World Intellectual Property Organization reported 1,456 cases. In 2020, the number of cases was 4,204.

If these findings confirm the preliminary idea, it will be possible to establish the "reasons to start up"[59], according to the new business "Vision" and "Mission". Otherwise, entrepreneurs should adjust expectations to match the likely results[60].

Although these concepts may change over time, we must consider them from the beginning to create a frame that limits our planning.

---

59 Tiffany P, Peterson S, Barrow C, "Business Plans for Dummies" 3rd ed. John Wiley and Sons 2012
60 Croneberger Jen, "Difference between Purpose, Mission and Vision" Forbes Magazine, Mar 04, 2020. https://www.forbes.com/sites/forbescoachescouncil/2020/03/04/vision-mission-and-purpose-the-difference/?sh=2dfd6488280e

In case you have not completed it before, this is the time to review the legal framework related to the project. In doing so, it will be possible to identify the records, permits, formalities and duties required for the business constitution and start-up.

Likewise, the entrepreneur will identify the legal procedures needed for shielding the intellectual property or rights linked to the project. Additionally, it is important to determine legal provisions that limit or condition the operation and trading of the product/service[61].

It is desirable that ideas, information, and analysis collected throughout the planning exercise be arranged in a "Descriptive Summary". It is a document that thematically exposes the business essentials[62].

Invisible barriers.

Entry and exit barriers are rarely considered by entrepreneurs. On the one hand, operational scales, technical requirements and extreme competition are usually factors that complicate entry into some markets. On the other hand, the indebtedness and the execution of guarantees that could occur when leaving the business. In any case, we suggest including them in your analysis.

Once these steps are completed, entrepreneurs will have established the project pre-feasibility, thus confirming that the product/service can be created/provided, because there are no limitations or barriers to offering it.

Likewise, entrepreneurs should have a hypothesis about potential clients and the reasons they will demand the product/service. These are references that will feed the marketing plan.

With these starting points, it will be possible to work on the scope, difficulty, and cost of the analysis of our business operation, which is the second objective of this long planning exercise.

b. From checking project viability to design the operation

Regardless that entrepreneurs have the experience required to develop the product or provide the service, they must design the business operation.

---

61 Bagley Constance, Dauchy Graig "The entrepreneur's guide to Law and strategy" Cengage Learning Fifth edition 2018,

62 This Summary should describe the product/service, its market, relevant aspects of the operation, development times and, if possible, a review of the products/services that compete with ours. This document will evolve during the entrepreneurship process until it becomes a "Business Plan".

Here, we refer to a detailed description of what should happen in the business, describing what, where when and how it would operate. Such a plan must detail the processes, as well as the resources that make them possible, which means describing elements such as times, personnel, machinery, networks, installations, access to services, procedures, controls, qualities, and other issues.

Because of this design, it is possible to quantify key magnitudes related to important operative factors, such as the inputs volume, the manufacturing capacity, or the planned service scale, among others.

This exercise, unlike the preliminary one, considers a detailed and well-supported work by suppliers and reliable sources of information that identify the capabilities, processes, and specifications involved in the operation. This review is essential to prepare the investment and expense budgets that will feed the subsequent project's financial evaluation.

Sites

A broad concept of site should include besides facilities (physical locations), the websites and any domains or active social media accounts. This is especially true when part of the marketing or advertising plans use these means.

Once we identify the scale, nature, and quality of the operation, we must define the work team in terms of number of employee and professional profiles. Both variables will help budget the payroll, but also planning the hiring and induction processes[63].

After designing the operation, entrepreneurs must organize the business administration and control, which usually includes the records of transactions and accountability, assets control, compliance, legal duties and managing the stakeholders, among others.

Finally, it is necessary to define the workplace conditions. Here we refer to the physical characteristics of the premises, shed or office where to create work areas, warehouses, refrigeration areas, workshop areas, among others. Likewise, the tasks related to the Web or Blog design must be included in this list of pending exercises to integrally design the "site".

---

63 De Silva Kimberly, “5 Best Practices for Hiring Superior Employees for Your Startup” Entrepreneur Magazine. Feb 2018 https://www.entrepreneur.com/business-news/5-best-practices-for-hiring-superior-employees-for-your/308439

c. From the operation design to the market positioning

On par with the design of the operation, we need to identify the industry and the market(s) in which we take part. This will offer us references on the customer niche(s) that would demand our product/service.

Completing a market research

An irrefutable proof of your market research's quality is the identification of products/services that compete directly or indirectly with yours. Likewise, the identification of similar products/services in other markets. Be careful to be surprised by someone who corrects your findings.

Dealing with this issue requires sufficient and reliable data to identify the size, evolution, and composition of the market, as well as the references to segment it.

Identifying segments helps us to recognize the potential demand of the different consumers/users' groups in terms of qualities/utilities and prices/rates.

Understanding the customers' preference according to the relationship between their profile and the existing offer in the market makes easier to position our offer based on a well-planned differentiation.

To confirm our client profile, we must research the group where consumers may belong[64]. In this investigation, we will identify tastes and preferences, and the willingness to consume/use our product/service.

Next, we design the research tools, as well as the subsequent collection, organization, and study of opinions. Keep in mind that the research must identify our product/service attributes, and the optimal price/quality/utility ratio according to the group surveyed[65].

Market research

Over 80% of the entrepreneurs who used ENTREPREVIEW® did not know how to carry out a market research, nor the usefulness of the data they can get from this activity.

For most entrepreneurs, these exercises are mandataries, since market research carried out by specialized firms may be unaffordable. However, homemade investigations may offer reliable conclusions as long as they

64 This research must aim a representative population sample with statistical significance. There are dozens of sources that explain this exercise. To identify them, we suggest consulting: https://en.wikipedia.org/wiki/Survey_sampling

65 A good introduction at: https://en.wikipedia.org/wiki/Survey_methodology

comply with technical standard when selecting the sample. Hence, we obtain an unbiased opinion about the attractiveness of our offer.

Regardless of the research alternative, entrepreneurs must always attempt to connect with the potential consumers to get evidence that will help design a comprehensive marketing plan. Here, we refer to a plan that includes a strategy to promote and advertise the product/service and defines the most effective distribution channels to serve the target group[66].

d. From market positioning to financial feasibility

This is a key objective in designing a viable and competitive strategy for our business.

The first step is to identify the income and expenses as products of the planned operation.

Regarding income, entrepreneurs must analyze the information obtained from market analyses and compare their product/service with that of their competitors, to reach a plausible price/rate range.

Such price/rate must be consistent with the quantities that will potentially sell, considering the capacity to produce or offer the product/service, as well as the marketing plan designed to increase the customer base that originally justified the business.

We must adjust the gross sales forecasting to the discounts and margins of the distribution channels, sales, transportation, and storage expenses, as well as the promotion and advertising costs. If we also consider the delivery and collection policies to be established with the sales/distribution network, it will be possible to determine the actual income.

On the other hand, we must foresee the business expenses, which includes those that belong to the ordinary operation, its administration, and control. Likewise, we must consider purchases (i.e., investment) of the goods and services required to lead the operation to the projected scale.

---

66 There are hundreds of books on marketing and merchandising. The last one I reviewed was written by Robert Palmatier, Shrihari Sridhar, "Marketing Strategy: Based on First Principles and Data Analytics" – Red Globe Press; 1st edition, 2017

New companies' bankruptcy

More frequent reasons for closing a new company: lack of money; wrong price definition; no knowledge about sources of financing; omissions in the planning process.

These estimations must be complemented by quantifying the credits that we can obtain from different suppliers, as well as the implicit investment when changing the inventories sizes.

Next, we should build an income and expenses budget to estimate the likely demand of money for a defined period[67].

The simple difference of income and expenses would offer a good reference of the amount to finance, if needed. However, here we recommend projecting these accounts over a foreseeable horizon (e.g., two or three years), under a convenient frequency (e.g., monthly). This detailed projection will help us estimate the business liquidity level, under certain scenarios, very useful to measure the short and medium-term financing, if required. With these elements, it is possible to design a realistic Capital Structure[68] for our business.

In line with the above, figure 5.3 presents a classification of the basic financing alternatives, whose availability will depend on the government financing programs; the financial institutions and the legal framework that regulates them; the private initiatives to promote entrepreneurship, and even of the real possibilities of the partners to fund their project.

Once we define the accounts that explain the inflows and cash outflows over time, as well as the sources of financing to cover the deficits, we can calculate a tentative business value. The standard procedure is to design a reliable/consistent scenario[69] and defining a reasonable discount rate.

---

67 Daly Lyle." The Complete Guide to Budgeting Methods" The ascent magazine. Jul 2021. https://www.fool.com/the-ascent/banks/articles/complete-guide-budgeting-methods/. Be sure to review the Microsoft templates to create budgets in a spreadsheet. https://templates.office.com/es-es/presupuestos

68 This term identifies the combination of debt, capital and pseudo capital that finances the company's operation. Brealey, R. and Myers, S. Principles of Corporate Finance. McGraw-Hill.

69 This is another topic covered in hundreds of books. I suggest reading articles to familiarize yourself with the different perspectives about the subject. Shoemaker Paul J., "Scenario Planning: A Tool for Strategic Thinking" MITS loan Management Review, Winter 1995

Figure 5.3
New companies financing alternatives

Although we would be ready to estimate a present value, we recommend not making a business decision yet. For now, the value we got will serve as a reference to adjust strategies and negotiate the required financing. Only after the potential creditors/partners confirm their willingness to take part in the business we will make our decision to invest and organize it. This step is key in all entrepreneurship and therefore we explain it next.

e. From financial feasibility to partnership setup

After identifying the financing sources that could meet business needs, entrepreneurs must build the most convenient capital structure[70].

To achieve this goal, it is necessary to study the way to contact those agents willing to invest their resources, either as partners, sponsors, or simple creditors.

If conditions and luck exist to access these financing sources, then we must choose only the convenient alternatives in terms of profitability, repayment, and maturity[71].

---

70 Robb, Alicia and Robinson, David T., The Capital Structure Decisions of New Firms (February 11, 2009). Disponible en SSRN: https://ssrn.com/abstract=1345895
71 We deal with this financing issue in the case study "Automotive Service Center," available at www.esp.entrepreview.net, in the section "Riskless Entrepreneurship".

Thus, the process begins by contacting entities and people within your network. In doing so, we will determine, among other factors, the possibilities, and restrictions of each source to finance our project; the costs and returns they demand (i.e., interest, expenses, commissions, profitability); procedures required to formalize any agreement, as well as the conditions to repay credits or contributions.

This investigation must also detect the genuine interest of these sources in financing our project, as well as the most relevant factors they consider in their analyzes and decisions[72]. Based on this information, entrepreneurs can weight advantages and disadvantages of each financing source. (Table 5.4).

Sources	Advantages	Disadvantages
Own Capital	• The management is autonomous deciding plans and business priorities. Low levels of indebtedness.	• Own resources are usually limited. All risks are assumed. No credit record is created
Third party Capital	• Risks are shared. Synergies likelihood. Make easier further financing.	• Consensus is necessary. Partners will demand higher accountability. Partners do not always add value.
Refundable loans	• Funding is cheaper. Risks are shared. A well-leveraged company multiplies chances to grow.	• Guarantees must be offered. Repayments are usually rigid. Debts increase insolvency or illiquidity risk.
Unrefundable loans	• Free financing. The bankruptcy risk disappears. Make easier funding from other sources, increasing the chances of growing.	• They are difficult to get. They are usually "small amounts". Occasionally imposes equity and operating restrictions that may limit options to develop the business

Table 5.4
Financing sources advantages and disadvantages[73]

Next, we should prepare a project presentation adjusted to the expectations or requirements of every potential finance source. The document that par excellence meets this requirement is called "Business Plan." It collects the results of the studies, analyzes and evaluations carried out concerning the project.

When dealing to this document, we are not only referring a considerable amount of data and information that we must get, organize, and present professionally. We also talk about the conclusions offered by the studies, analyzes and exercises made to determine the project attractiveness.

---

72 With project competitions, very common in recent years, the research that must be completed is very similar to the one suggested.

73 This is a partial list, since it does not include, for example, governmental programs loans that exist in many countries. See the case of Canada Small Business Financing Program, at http://www.ic.gc.ca/eic/site/csbfp-pfpec.nsf/eng/Home

Keep in mind that this report will support the arguments that you will tackle when selling your business to your counterparts and, therefore, its integrity is essential[74].

Good Business Plan

Alternatives to complete a soundness Business Plan: 1) Professional support; 2) Be trained in a business matters (e.g., to get a MBA) ; 3) Find an experienced partner; 4) Promote only businesses that already have a plan made (e.g., franchises)

Along with your Business Plan, there is an exercise that deserves special attention at this phase. Not only because of the time and energy that it will demand, but it will be the subject of debate when presenting your project to each finance source. Here we refer to the "Value Proposal".

This proposal should not only refer to the profitability (i.e. value) that will compensate for the risks of investing in the project. You must also specify the financing conditions your project requires in terms of the money, costs, guarantees, and repayment conditions.

Recognizing what it is expected and what it is offered from each side of the negotiation table is an excellent step to overcome the typical "opposition of interests" in this type of agreement. Table 5.5 summarizes the "ideal conditions" for each of the parties, where we can observe the paradox that this type of negotiation entails.

Note that each party's conditions usually are the same but defined from an opposite point of view. That is, each party seeks business control, the highest profitability, and the least possible risk.

Given the number of details to consider in these negotiations, entrepreneurs must prepare flexible scenarios to adapt the business to possible deals conditions. Such flexibility may change investment plans, operation scale and repayment plans[75].

¿? Value is a guarantee?

For a bank, is it better to fund projects with positive present value or covering the loan with real guarantees?

74 There are dozens of Web sites and applications that offer business plan design services, some of them very complete and totally tutored.

75 There are many other factors to consider. Cremades Alejandro, "The art of startup fundraising" John Wiley and Sons, 2016

Entrepreneurs must define ranges for the key conditions to avoid accepting a risky financing that implies repayment terms beyond the business' capability, reimbursements not aligned to the business needs, or financing that leads the founders' shareholding dilution.

Ideal financing conditions for starting a business?	Ideal conditions to invest/lend resources for a project?
Sufficient: The source of funding should meet the todays and future' funds requirements.	**Sufficient:** Financing shouldn't exceed the investment budgets designed for the type, size, and risk of the business.
Controllable: The sources of financing must be compatible with the business plan and the foreseen business equity control.	**Controllable:** Financing should not prevent the control of basic aspects of the business, such as investments, leverage, and profits distribution.
Profitable: The cost per financing should be the lowest possible and never higher than the partners' expected yield.	**Profitable:** The project's IRR should be higher than the expected return from the financing sources.
Free of risk: Contributions or loans should not demand personal guarantees from promoters or establish limitations according to the business results.	**Free of risk:** There should be assets that guarantee the investment/loan if the project does not achieve the expected results.
Repayable: The financing should be affordable according to the business possibilities.	**Repayable:** Financing must be recovered from the company's cash flow within the agreed period.

Table 5.5
Every table side's ideal business financing conditions.

We acknowledge the fact that, for many entrepreneurs, that loan or contribution are vital, since without these funds the project simply would not exist. However, keep in mind that financing is not a fulfilled premise, but an element that we must explore and plan for when determining the business viability. In other words, financing cannot be understood as a fait accompli, nor can it be assumed at any cost or under any repayment condition. It is simply an element that we must carefully evaluate before making a business decision.

Only after establishing the business feasibility, defining a strategy that increases our chances and agreeing on the financing conditions, then it is the ideal time for the entrepreneur to create "the company"[76].

---

76 We use these terms because it is not always about constituting a corporation. Sometimes, for example, a non-profit foundation or even a partnership (e.g., LLC or SRL) could be better adjusted to the contribution of the sponsors.

This last step supposes the fulfillment of all the duties/formalities, which includes, among others, the legal entity registration, the formal capitalization of contributions, and register the board meeting minutes in the company books.

Likewise, the company's authorities must be designated (i.e., directors, commissioners). They will control the business, represent the company, and approve the financial statements.

¿? Ideal partner?

Desirable qualities for a new partner: 1) large experience in the business' critical subjects; 2) wealthy enough; 3) linked to networks that can aggregate value; 4) trustworthy person; 5) fully devoted to the project.

For the strategic phase purposes, the above process would be the culminating step. The formalization of a profitable initiative for those who invest in it.

Please note that alteration or omission of any critical step may be inconvenient since our decision to go ahead with the business would be premature, exposing partners to participate in an unfair deal. Because of its importance, we will further insist on this point.

5.2 The Pre-operation

When focusing on the Pre-operational phase, we can identify in all businesses three objectives to fulfill: business assembling, hiring the staff, and complying with the legal duties and operational requisite (See Figure 5.6).[77]

Business assembling refers to the organization and setup of the operations already planned up.

This objective goes from the selection, formal possession, and adaptation of a facility where the business will operate to creating the website for advertising and selling the good or service being offer.

Consequently, this list includes the purchase and reception of the supply, equipment, furniture, machinery, tools, and other assets involve in

77 Attachment B presents a list of the activities that usually make up the processes of the Pre-Operational phase. These lists should be adapted for each type of business, just as the ENTREPRE-VIEW® does.

the operation. Also, consider the work of installing, assembling, and setting them up.

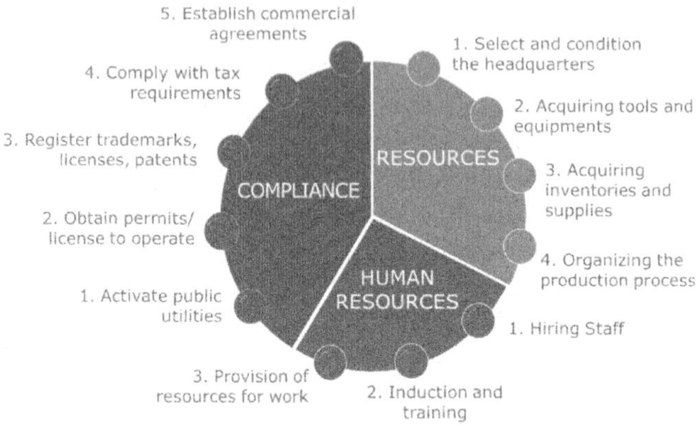

Figure 5.6
Pre-Operative processes and objectives
Case: Manufacturing business

The second objective refers to the processes to build the work-team. Here we talk about the hiring, induction and training of the personnel who will work in the different business areas[78].

Finally, we must deal with the processes that fulfill formal duties. This objective includes all tasks required to get registrations, patents, permits and licenses necessary to operate.

Likewise, we must consider the formalities behind the agreements and commitments between the business and its "stakeholders".

Employee-partners

When integrally evaluating the creation of a company, do not forget that key employees are also part of the partnership, whether or not they have a company shareholding.

When reviewing the processes that fulfill each objective, we realize that their correct execution is based on a well-elaborated plan, which identifies the goods and services to incorporate, as well as a logical sequence of the tasks to efficiently assemble this gigantic puzzle.

78 Among useful papers and articles, I read: Chamorro Premuzic, Tomas, "3 Emerging Alternatives to Traditional Hiring Methods", Harvard Business Review, June 26, 2015. https://hbr.org/2015/06/3-emerging-alternatives-to-traditional-hiring-methods

It is common that, after a period between planning and carrying out the pre-operation, some conditions change, which forces us to adjust the budget, work schedule or both. For such circumstances, it is necessary to search effective antidotes to mitigate the impact of these modifications.

The more effective is to accept that changes will always occur. To consider them reasonably in our planning, it is necessary to define ranges or margins when preparing our plans and budgets[79].

Defining these margins is not a trivial task. In fact, it demands applying scarce intangibles: good criteria and experience. Therefore, our suggestion is to consult with professionals with the "know-how" to create plans and establish margins that deal with contingencies.

The other condition that we cannot ignore before conducting the pre-operation is to complete all the steps that feed the decision to start the business.

As already explained, we bias our decision to venture when we invest or partner with third parties before going to the process we described above. It exposes us to wasting time, effort, and money in an uncertain business.

¿? Scenarios design

What safety margin is recommended to consider when designing scenarios? Adopting other point of view, what scenario do we value our business? The most probable, the conservative, or the optimistic?

Explained in this way, the suggested sequence should be obvious to many. However, most entrepreneurs do not follow the proposed order. By ignoring the milestones that establish the beginning and the end of these preliminary phases, we are not only playing down the role of each process. We also underestimate the importance of getting reliable evidence during our planning.

Given the importance to meet this condition, we are going to dedicate the following chapter to explain the link between the different processes of our entrepreneurship stage. It will be a preface of chapter seven, where we expose the concept of "consistency" which is critical for the risk control that we can adopt during our entrepreneurship exercise.

---

79 The great secret to anticipate assertively is to assume that there will always be alterations to our plan. Whether the typical "optimism" of our suppliers, or the adjustments we usually make to our plans, or because of unforeseeable errors and omissions, we must always plan with the certainty that the business will require more money, effort and time than expected.

Chapter 6. Interdependency

When discovering the interrelation between the entrepreneurship processes, we identify the must-exercises relevance, and the problems that may arise if we do not perform them.

After presenting Risk Control fundamentals and explain the strategic stage scope, in this chapter we will consider a third element related to the planning of a reliable strategy.

Remember that we have defined the strategic phase as the future business genesis, where we do the research to collect helpful evidence to plan a sound business project. Such planning must establish operational details and projected results that confirm the business' attractiveness. Depending on the promised results, it will be possible/desirable to invite investors/lenders to finance the business and make a reasonable profit.

We also insist that this planning must consider the Risk Control point of view, since it is not enough to define conditions to operate and grow. In addition, we must reduce the risk of the business evolution.

Such an approach means completing a planning exercise that identifies the quantity and quality of the resources that the business requires operating safely.

Too much optimism

A common source of errors when planning is to consider the optimal result to get, instead of focus our actual possibilities. The idea is to handle our expectations, especially when we deal with a novel project.

Now we are interested in considering an additional element in our analysis that helps us further reduce risks. It is about the interdependence between the entrepreneurship phases' processes.

When planning, we must consider this condition to promote a consistent strategy. In other words, the idea is to build a feasible business strategy in certain contexts, with the available resources.

Given the importance of achieving coherence between a wide range of variables, this chapter will explain another way to accomplish our entrepreneurship exercise. That is, to work on our business strategy's consistency and determine how realistic are the foreseeable results.

6.1 Interdependency

Reliability of an analysis and planning processes is not only achieved by getting the most reliable information and using of the most complete technique to accomplish analysis and calculation. The idea is also getting data and evidence that does not contradict each other. In other words, we must use consistent information.

To achieve such consistency, entrepreneurs must consider the interdependence between the tasks to accomplish. That is, to realize that every exercise is preceded by others, whose results must be considered if the idea is to reach a coherent planning exercise.

These dependencies, very common in complex planning processes, are illustrated in Table 6.1.

Factor to determine	Factors to consider
Production capacity	Product + supplies + installation + technology + labor
Production	Production capacity + working capital
Unitary cost	Production + foreseen cost/expenses
Sale's price	Unitary cost + Margin + competition prices + positioning
Foreseen sales	Sale's Price +Distribution channel+ advertising + promotions
Foreseen inflows	Forseen sales + collections + sales expenses
Cash flow	Forseen inflows + Forseen outflows + financing
Value	Cash Flow + Cost of capital + business strategy

Table 6.1
Interdependency between exercises of the planning process.
Case: Manufacturing company

It shows the factors to consider sequentially when determining, for example, the "Project Value" which, as we know, is a key result of our business planning.

The sequence illustrates the different variables and evidence we may incorporate into complex calculations and analyses. Although we can start this sequence from the very basic tasks, in this example we started it with the definition of "Production Capacity"[80].

As shown, the calculation of this factor considers the type of product to manufacture, the inputs, the plant capacity, the machinery, equipment, as well as the workforce.

80 We can determine this variable after planning the product to manufacture, the required inputs, the installation of our workshop or factory, the required technology, and the required workforce.

In turn, this factor will be a variable when estimating the expected "Production", which is also considered in the Unit Costs calculation, and is a mandatory reference when defining the Sale Price, and so on.

This "cascade effect" illustrates, on the one hand, the omnipresence of some factors in business planning (e.g., costs, sale price). On the other hand, it highlights the attention we must take on the links between the factors involved in our business' planning.

Unfortunately, most entrepreneurs do not take these relations into account, which leads to omissions that weaken our planning reliability.

Inconsistency (examples)

- Planning sales that exceed distribution capacity.
- Offering a service that relies on hard-to-find supplies.
- Projecting the results of complex operations, considering non-competitive salaries.

As typical examples, we might refer to the sale price that does not adjust to the quality perceived by potential clients, or the advertising plan that does not match the target consumer preferences[81].

It can then be concluded that the execution, as well as the order to carry out our planning exercises, seems to play a crucial role in the strategic phase results. This would lead us to design a work map whose order reinforces these relationships.

Unfortunately, the accomplishment of a strategic plan that follows a specific order will not always be possible because, among other facts, the information accessibility does not fit any script. That is why entrepreneurs must work a posteriori on data consistency to feed the business planning without having major setbacks.

6.2 Dependency between processes

We have already explained that activities that comprise the processes of the strategic and pre-operational phases are interdependent. It means that they depend on and feed the rest of the processes. Let us explain this last statement.

---

81 Not considering the logical order to accomplish the Pre-operation phase can also be inconvenient. I have witnessed entrepreneurs who design a complete production process without having confirmed the availability of facility with the capacity to house the machinery, personnel, and other work elements.

Although each process responds to a specific objective, much of the information that they have produced feeds not only the process itself but other processes. The typical case is the activities comprised the "Planning of the productive process", which is part of the second objective of the strategic phase or "Design of the Operation Model" (See Figure 6.2).

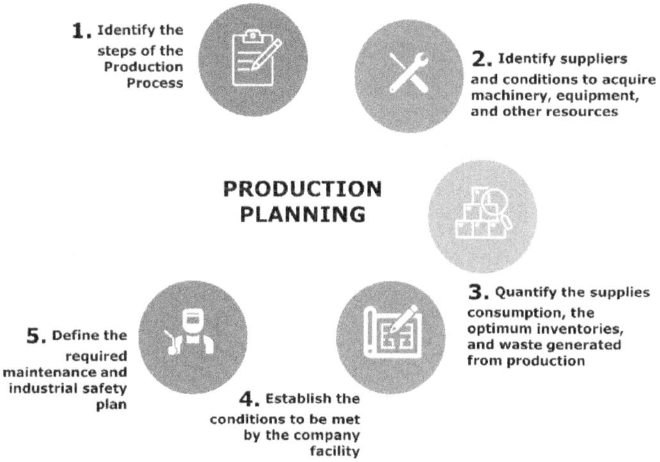

Figure 6.2
"Operational planning" activities.
Case: Manufacturing company

As its name suggests, the idea of this process is to plan details of the operation, which includes, among others, designing the workflow, identifying the machinery and equipment, defining the type and quantity of raw materials, establishing workplace conditions, selecting suppliers, as well as defining controls and security policies.

If you look closely, activities that make this process possible are sequential, because the information got during each activity feeds the following ones

This is, for example, the reason we cannot decide the machinery and equipment to use (i.e., activity 2), without establishing the manufacturing process (i.e., activity 1). Similarly, we cannot select a facility (i.e., activity 3) without first defining the machinery and equipment to be used, and so on. Again, dependency could condition the order in which to accomplish our analyses.

The other consequence is the use of the information we collect during the process. When we design the manufacturing process, important data are derived, such as the production capacity, as well as the selection of some assets that must be purchased.

Both factors will be references to determining key variables. We are referring, on the one hand, to the amount of product to offer, which defines the maximum sales volume. On the other hand, the purchase of fixed assets, is a key variable when defining the total investment, the required financing, and the business value.

Our planning assumptions

By omitting analyzes or research that provide/confirm critical information, we weaken our planning. These gaps can only be filled, at best, with assumptions.

Only when considering these two variables (i.e., the amount of product to offer and the fixed assets purchase), we may infer "Planning the productive process" that also feeds two more processes: "Total Income" and "Total Expenditures".

Additionally, "Planning of the productive process" feeds other vital processes, such as "Definition of the work team", "Planning the business' administration and control ", and "Planning the distribution and sales model" (See Matrix 6.3).

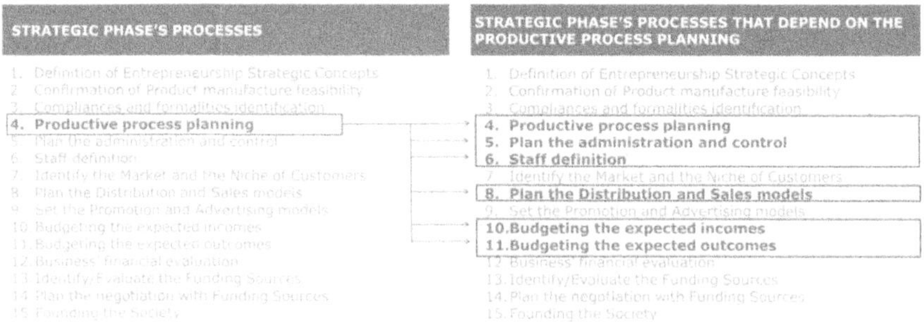

Matrix 6.3

Dependency between "Productive process planning" and other strategic phase processes. Case: Manufacturing company

We reiterate the importance of considering this dependency when executing each of the strategic phase processes. In this way, we will know the reason for completing each exercise, which helps to understand the consistency required in our analyses.

Please note the fact that such consistency contributes to the definition of a "coherent project". It explains why consistency is an effective antidote to avoid weaknesses from our planning, which is an essential part of the Risk Control in this phase.

For control purpose, note that dependency exists throughout the strategic phase processes, as evidenced in Matrix 6.4. When reviewing this table, we find peculiarities worth analyzing.

	Strategic phase processes influenced by the same phase processes' accomplishment														
Strategic phase processes that influence the same phase processes' accomplishment	Entrepreneurship's key concepts.	Feasibility to build and operate the business.	Identify the formal and legal duties	Planning the business operation	Plan administration and control.	Staff planning	Market positioning	Plan merchandising /trading model.	Advertising and promotions planning.	Estimating inflows, and outflows	Determine financing requirements.	Financial Evaluation	Identify the financing sources conditions.	Negotiate with financing sources.	Founding your partnership.
Entrepreneurship's key concepts.	x	x	x	x	x	x	x	x	x	x	x	x	x	x	x
Feasibility to build and operate the business.	x	x		x		x	x	x	x	x	x	x	x	x	x
Identify the formal and legal duties	x	x	x	x	x	c	x	x	c	x	x	x	c	c	c
Planning the business operation	x	x	x	x	x	c	x	x	c	x	x	x			
Plan the administration and control.	x		x	c	x	x				x		x		x	x
Staff planning	x	x	x	x	x	x	x	x		x		x			x
Market positioning	x	x	c	x		x	x	x	x	x		x			
Plan the merchandising/trading model.	x	x	x	x	x	x	x	x	x	x		x			
Advertising and promotions planning.	x		x				x	x	x	x		x			
Estimating inflows, and outflows	x			x	x	x	x	x	x	x	x	x	x	x	
Determine financing requirements.	x			x			x			x	x	x	x	x	
Financial Evaluation	x	x		x			x	x		x	x	x	x	x	x
Identify the financing sources availabilty/conditions.	x	x		x			x	x		x	x	x	x	x	x
Negotiate with financing sources.	x		x		x					x	x	x	x	x	x
Founding your partnership.	x		x		x	x				x		x	x		x

Matrix 6.4
Dependency between the Strategic phase's processes

First, all processes depend on themselves because every one of their activities defines conditions essential to accomplishing the rest of the activities.

This relation even applies to those processes where activities complement each other. Note that the mere aim of achieving an acceptable consistency defines certain links with their sister activities.

On the other hand, the first process on the list, "Definition of the business and formulation of strategic concepts", includes an important activity (i.e., Mission and Objectives definition). These very basic concepts are linked to all the studies and calculations of the planning phase, defining their qualitative and quantitative goals. Therefore, the first process on the list is a mandatory reference for the rest of the processes.

Finally, there are relationships that could be "conditioned", as it occurs with the process "A census of formalities and compliances".

The proceedings, records, and applications comprised there might not only legally authorize the business operation. Corresponding legal frame may also condition operations, as occurs, for example, with the "Planning of the work team".

¿? Omitting duties

If we start an undercover business, should we review the legal framework and understand the duties to comply? What about the processes derived from such duties? Do we carry them out without considering the time and costs involved?

A good example happens when businesses must hire impaired people[82], or a limited number of foreign employees. Since not all legal frames may condition these and other business elements, we suggest using them as conditional.

We invite readers to become familiar with this matrix to understand some conditions that should not be ignored when establishing dependencies at their entrepreneurship exercise.

6.3 Dependency between the Strategic and Pre-Operative phases

The Strategic phase processes have obvious relationships with the pre-Operative ones. It is so since the very reason for the first phase is to provide the planning and financing that the second phase requires.

To highlight this relationship, we built a new table (See Matrix 6.5.) like the previous one.

82 Similar conditions are considered in countries such as Spain, Mexico, Bolivia, Argentina, Brazil, and Venezuelans legal frameworks.

Strategic phase processes that influence the Pre operational processes' accomplishment	Pre Operational phase processes influenced by the strategic phase processes accomplishment.									
	Set up the administration and control unit	Obtain licenses, permits, and comply with legal duties	Create the business web site	Tenure or legal occupancy of the plot/premises/local.	Conditioning the facility/workplace	Acquire/install furniture and equipment	Purchase supplies/inventories to the business	Staff recruitment, induction and endowment	Activate commercializing /sales channels	Launch the advertising/promo plans
Entrepreneurship's key concepts.	x	x	x	x	x	x	x	x	x	x
Feasibility to build and operate the business.				x	x	x	x	x		
Identify the formal and legal duties	x	x	x	c	c	c		c		c
Planning the business operation	x	x	x	x	x	x	x	x	x	x
Plan the administration and control.	x		x		x	x				
Staff planning	x	c		x	x	x		c		
Market positioning			x	x					x	x
Plan the merchandising/trading		x	x	x				x	x	x
Advertising and promotions planning.		c	x	c					x	c
Estimating inflows. and outflows	x			x	x	x	x	x	x	x
Determine financing requirements.		x								
Financial Evaluation		x				x	x			x
Identify the financing sources		x								
Negotiate with financing sources.										
Founding your partnership.	x	x	x	x	x	x	x	x	x	x

Matrix 6.5
Dependency between Strategic phase's processes
and pre Operative phase's processes

In this table, there are unambiguous links, as it happens with the "Activation of the administration and control entities", a process that depends on the planning of the areas included in the strategic phase (i.e., "Plan the administration and control of the business").

Other links are numerous, as we see in the "Contact customers and send samples". This process depends on both the "Identification of the market niche" and the "Planning of the distribution and sales models" included in the strategic phase.

A more complex case is presented in the process "Select and formalize the occupancy and use of the facility". As seen in Matrix 6.6, this process depends on others that, individually, bring references or condition to select the right site.

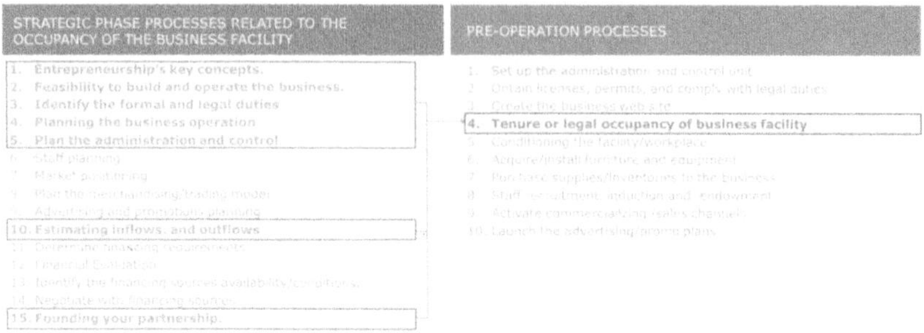

Matrix 6.6
Dependency between the "Selection and formalize the business facility" and strategic phase's processes

The latter multiplicity is explained because the "selection of the workplace" must be compatible with the planning of the production process and the selection of the work team. In addition, entrepreneurs must consider other aspects of the operation often under regulations, as well as the best location to distribute and sell.

Again, we recommend considering the activities involved in each process, to understand the dependency stated in the attached tables. Identifying these relationships will help to understand the relevance of the processes and the weaknesses created from omissions or deficiencies in the planning process.

6.4 Work plan order

Let us add a final idea regarding the way to make the entrepreneurship execution more flexible, aware of the entrepreneurs' difficulties in getting reliable information about the project and its contexts.

So far, we have proposed dividing the entrepreneurship stage into two different phases (i.e., strategic, and pre-operational). We have also stated that the pre-operational phase can only be started after obtaining the required financing (i.e., end of the strategic phase). Doing it differently would increase the risk of losing all the effort, money, and other resources we might invest (i.e., high-risk entrepreneurship).

As seen, during the strategic phase, we have proposed to meet five specific objectives, according to a sequence that we restate in Figure 6.7, that shows the dependence of each of the objectives.

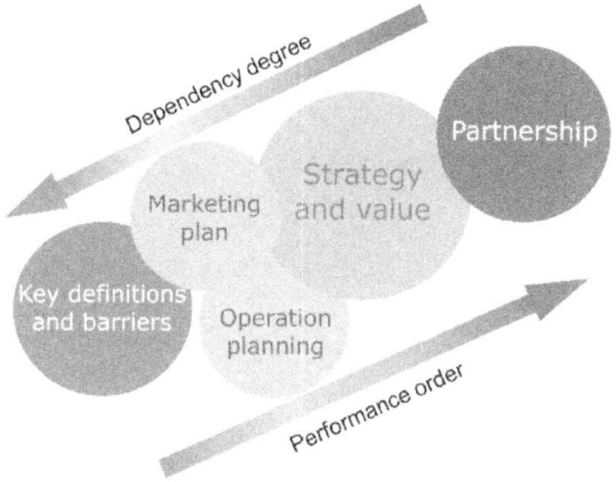

Figure 6.7
Strategic phase's objectives.
Original execution's order and dependency

Found an adequate financed business is only possible if we first design/propose a strategy that creates value.

The value estimation is based on our business operations, which considers how we operate and sell. The underlying business strategy must respond, not only to the reasons for starting up. It must also be consistent with a business mission and vision.

As explained, to meet these objectives, demands to accomplish a set of processes and activities considered in the strategic phase. However, by presenting them in a list, we are unintentionally suggesting a sequence to execute them.[83].

Indeed, it will always be necessary to follow some work sequences that have already been exposed. However, we insist that the probability of complying according to a desired sequence is relatively low. The good news is that we can start our strategic exercise with the process of any objective without reducing the reliability of our findings.[84]

---

83 The suggested order should increase planning consistency.

84 After learning the interdependence between the strategy exercise, it will be difficult to accept any business plan. This means working more than usual before deciding about our business.

We illustrate this condition in Figure 6.8, where we avoid indicating any starting point for planning (i.e., specific objectives). We show the processes to accomplish, in a sort of a centrifuge that ends with the decision to carry out or not the project.

Figure 6.8
Alternative flowchart to complete the strategic phase

According to this outline, it seems to be the same to start, for instance, "designing the current operation", or "positioning the product/service". Moreover, starting with the ending processes (e.g., review potential financing sources) can be a more abstract, but effective alternative if we prefer to order a long and complex exercise.

As explained in the next chapter, the fundamental condition for managing planning flexibly is to "quarantine" each piece of information until confirm its consistency with the rest of the elements.

It is possible to measure and compare this consistency using metrics, simple to quantify, but very effective in controlling the risks of our business from its planning workflow. Let us see how these metrics work.

Chapter 7.
Monitoring the entrepreneurship

When planning a business, we strive to design a coherent strategy whose feasibility will depend on our plan's consistency, integrity, and risk level.

Once we explain the strategic phase work-plan, it is necessary to understand how to control it. For this purpose, we must accomplish two tasks: first, to check if the planning exercise provides reliable information to make a business decision. Second, identify sources of risk that may affect the business setup and operation.

At this stage, we mainly handle data we get, group, compare, and transform, to get goals, values, and strategies. All this happens by performing activities that represent "the areas" of the strategic phase.

Reasons to planning

We perform a complete entrepreneurship process, not only to gather solid arguments to associate with potential partners and lenders. We also do it to convince ourselves about the new business's chances of success.

To reduce risk in these areas, entrepreneurs must complete each activity with the highest technical rigor possible. When establishing the quality of our exercises, we must handle concepts such as "the adequate technique", or "accuracy", attributes difficult to measure without a trained criterion on how and why to accomplish managerial exercises.

This is the topic we address in this chapter, by being confident of the proposed alternatives to control our planning will help us understand risks that may affect our new business.

7.1 Progress control

The first control on the strategic exercise is based on its execution. This execution is the quantification of the progress achieved in every process measured as a percentage[85]. This percentage is based on the number of completed activities, and the total number of activities, as suggested by Equation 7.1[86].

$$\%\ \text{PROGRESS}_{\text{PROCESS}} = \frac{\text{NUMBER OF ACTIVITIES COMPLETED}}{\text{NUMBER OF TOTAL ACTIVITIES}} \times 100\%$$

Equation 7.1
Formula to estimate the progress

85 When we speak of executed activities, we refer to the tasks, totally or partially accomplished, without questioning the technical rigor or the quality of the references or information we got.
86 This concept is also used to estimate the progress of an objective, based on its processes.

This formula can determine the progress of a process that depends on activities whose progress uses a binary scale, illustrated in Table 7.2

Process #1 activities	Finished	Unfinished
Definition of Entrepreneurship Strategic Concepts	○	●
Confirmation of Product manufacture feasibility	●	○
Compliances and formalities identification	●	○
Productive process planning	○	●
Plan the administration and control	●	○

Table 7.2
Example of progress of a five activities process.

Here, the assigned progress on the not accomplished activities is 0%, while the accomplished activities represent 100% progress. Thus, the progress of the entire process (i.e., three activities out of five), reaches 60%.

Though this procedure is very simple, it cannot assign partial progresses. For this reason, it is recommended to use a graduated scale to represent the tasks progress with a little more precision, as shown in Matrix 7.3

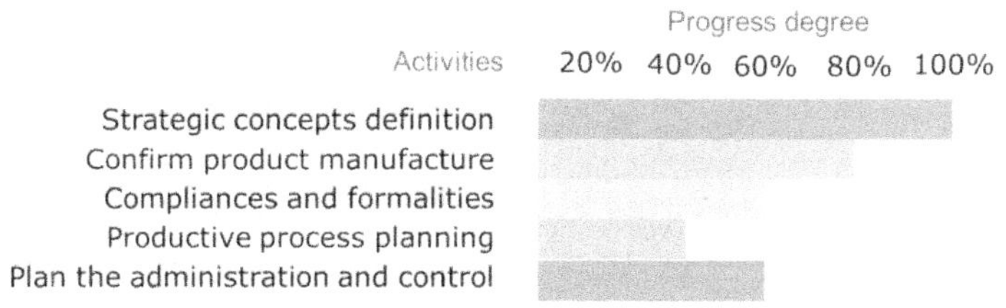

Matrix 7.3
A set of activities progress matrix.

As shown, the scale used makes it possible to quantify the partial progress of each activity. This way is very useful for controlling activities that require several tasks or different stages to be completed, which occur in most cases.

If considering this new scale, we must adjust equation 7.1 to estimate the average progress of our process, now assuming the partial progress for each activity. (See Equation 7.4)[87]

$$\%\ \text{PROGRESS}_{\text{PROCESS}} = \frac{\text{SUM ALL ACTIVITIES PROGRESS (\%)}}{\text{NUMBER OF ACTIVITIES}}$$

Equation 7.4
Progress formula calculation

There are more accurate versions for determining the average progress of a process. (e.g., geometric mean). In any case, the use of partial progress is more realistic for controlling complex strategic processes.

7.2 Quality control

Monitoring progress helps us to identify the activities/processes conducted along the entrepreneurship exercise. When we identify their progress, we must consider the technical rigor we followed for reaching realistic conclusions regarding our business.

This technical rigor implies using reliable sources of information and applying the correct technique to transform and analyze the data or evidence.

The underlying rule is to consider such conditions when quantifying progress. Therefore, we will consider as completed only those exercises that provide reliable evidence to support our business decision. Let's look at these transcendental conditions in more detail.

¿? Partial progress

One of the five steps to value our business is to design a model that projects expected cash flows. If the model is incomplete or too rigid to analyze business scenarios, what progress would you assign to the valuation exercise, assuming the rest of the evaluation activities as completed?

---

87 When applied to our example, the sum of the progresses is 340% (100% + 80% + 60% + 40% + 60%), which divided by 5 activities provides an average of 68% progress for the process.

a. Reliable information

Reliability is the degree to which a variable represents the condition or contexts of our business.

To manage representative information, we must use credible sources that account for the reality, event, or condition we analyze. These sources may have a different origin (i.e., primary, or secondary), nature (e.g., verbal, written), or formats (e.g., numeric, text). The important thing is to access truthful information to feed analyzes that help define reliable strategies[88].

To represent this condition, let's look at the case of an entrepreneur who seeks to define the rate to be charged for the information service he plans to launch. For this purpose, he will consult as many sources of information as possible until get credible evidence. To complete this exercise, he has defined a two phases work plan (See Table 7.5).

CASE	1. MARKET ANALYSIS	2. MARKET RESEARCH
Select the most complete procedure to define the subscription fee of the information service	Gathering market references and make comparisons to define a competitive fee. • Identify fee for similar services offered locally • Check fees in similar markets • Design the local the market fee-customers' curve to positioning every provider • Identify the differences between our service and the competitors' one • Consult with industry experts and players • Compare the latter fee with the corresponding with the business break-even point. • Determine the fee that guarantees a profit for different sales scenarios	Optionally, to carry out a field study to establish the acceptance of the fee got from the market analysis. • Analysis and definitions ○ Define the variables related to the fee service ○ Identify the user's profile ○ Select the sample • Poll/guided meeting design ○ Design the questionnaire or the guided meeting, to work with individuals or groups ○ Prepare informative material to supplement the questionnaire or the guided meeting ○ Hold the work sessions considering the expected time and information to collect

Table 7.5
Analysis to determine the fee of competitors' information services.
Analysis 2 involves confirming the Analysis 1 findings.

---

88 Redman Thomas C., "To Improve Data Quality, Start at the Source" Harvard Business Review. Feb10, 2020. https://hbr.org/2020/02/to-improve-data-quality-start-at-the-source

The first phase reviews the competitor's market position in which the service will take part. This means identifying, among others, the rates, the services, as well as the packages or promotions.

Though references from this investigation are unquestionable, they might not define the rate of the new service. This argument is especially true when we want to differentiate the service from the rest.

Hence, the entrepreneur can validate the findings by contacting a group of potential clients to understand their perception regarding the service's rates and scope. (Stage 2)

Research based on these primary sources guarantees reliable references for establishing the rate and the marketing plan to positions the service effectively.[89]

b. Applying the right technique

Our entrepreneur wants to perform field research that meets all the technical requirements. The problem is its cost and difficulty.

Indeed, fees of a specialized firm are high. Likewise, entrepreneurs often lack the capacity and resources to consult a significant group of potential users. This being the case, one might wonder if conducting a survey among friends and relatives is a valid-enough exercise to confirm these variables.

Without hesitation, the answer is affirmative since the information got in this manner will always be more representative than one's own opinion. However, one might wonder how to entrust this relevant business variable to a sample that lacks statistical significance.

> **¿? Partial progress**
>
> One of the five steps to value our business is to design a model that projects expected cash flows. If the model is incomplete or too rigid to analyze business scenarios, what progress would you assign to the valuation exercise, assuming the rest of the evaluation activities as completed?

Next, our entrepreneur must ask himself how to access the previously identified group. What are the issues to figure out in planned research? What tools are needed to collect and process opinions/surveys? And,

---

89 Smith, Scott "9 Key stages in your marketing research process" Dec7, 2020 https://www.qualtrics.com/blog/marketing-research-process/

finally, how reliable would these results be, considering the chosen indicators?

These and other practical questions must be formally addressed to accomplish a consultation according to marketing practices. Keep in mind, it is not about impulsive processes. It is about designing and applying queries, quantifications and analyzes consistent with this technical area.

By altering or omitting steps of the market research, we can misinterpret the received information, and considerably reducing its validity.

7.3 Consistency

In chapter six, we introduced the concept of "consistency", when explaining the dependency between the processes within the strategic phase.

We stated that such consistency was achieved when the execution of a process considers the largest number of variables that can influence it. The idea of considering this relation is to avoid innocent conclusions resulting from the inclusion in the same scenario variables and results that cannot coexist.

To review how to handle this criterion, let's go back to the example of launching the new information service. Remember that our definition of rates begins by researching companies that provide a similar service (i.e., Option 1). This review identifies their rates, services' scopes, and their subscribers' profiles, among others.

Whether we leave the exercise up to this point, the data we got must be temporary, since it is dependent on other revisions before "taking it for granted" in the business planning process.

Let's assume, for the purpose of these findings, that the identified average rate does not promise a generous profit margin in relation to the size and cost of our operation, which means the business value would be negative.

The first adjustment to implement would be to consider a higher service fee, increasing revenues, and rising both the operative margin and the corporate value.

Although there is no problem in adjusting our projections, in real life, such an increase cannot be arbitrary. In fact, there are market conditions that limit sales as a direct consequence of the rates.

Validating strategies

The present value is the perfect reference (i.e., pivot) to validate of all business strategies' veracity and consistency.

Suppose that we had to increase rates to guarantee a positive net value. This could, among other effects, leads us to create a more favorable offering that provides a higher value to users.

When talking about a more complete service (e.g., access to more information channels), it might be necessary to review, among others, the cost structure, because of the higher fees we must pay to providers to receive more channels or data.

In addition, we must confirm that customers will pay the new rate. Otherwise, we would have to reconsider our marketing plan by offering a competitive service geared towards a new customer niche.

This review, which must be accomplished step by step, could extend until we reassess all variables of our business. It supposes a not trivial multifactorial analysis (See Figure 7.7), since the evidence we may have regarding any variable suggests but also restricts other variables of our business scenarios.

Figure 7.7
Relations between the variables that help to define the services fee.

In this way, the definition of a business strategy does not imply that we can freely establish/change magnitudes. Rather, it recommends that we must comprehensively evaluate our business, which requires understanding the interdependence of the variables considered in the analyzes and calculations that feed our business decision.

7.4 Measuring consistency

The second reason to understand dependency between the variables comprised in a strategy would be their mutual consistency. Let us explain this condition step by step.

When studying consistency, we face a subject difficult to measure and apply since the tests and verifications seen in this chapter are based on well-trained criteria.

This is always the case because any exercise will have more than one way of accomplishing it. There will be more efficient but less exact procedures, as well as more exhaustive methods that require information difficult to collect.

Being aware of the wide range of ways for gathering reliable data and evidence, it is useful for entrepreneurs to weight the consistency of every exercise to establish how well supported their findings are.

> **i! Entrepreview®**
>
> The platform presents an entrepreneurship exercise archetype with the minimum number of activities required to evaluate and planning a new business.

Therefore, it is necessary to adopt a criterion for controlling our entrepreneurship process without ignoring difficulties involved in assessing the progress/completion of its exercises. We must also quantify the consistency based on the dependency between the different processes. The procedure for completing these steps is summarized as follows:

1. Identify the activities comprised your strategy to complete the processes. Matrices in Attachment A can help for this purpose.

2. For each process, identify all activities (i.e., their own and other processes) that can feed or condition it. An example of this match is shown in Table 7.8, that presents the activities linked to the administrative and control unit design.

3. Establish progress of each activity. Remember not label activities "as completed", unless they are accomplished according to the required technical accuracy, by accessing reliable sources of information.

Dependency example		
5. Design the administrative and control management.	1.5 Determine success factors.	100.0%
	3.2 Identify formal duties.	20.0%
	3.3 Identify formal duties requirements.	40.0%
	3.4 Identify the conditions/formalities with clients/suppliers.	20.0%
	3.6 Schedule future obligations/formalities.	100.0%
	5.1 Identify the reports required by the legal framework.	20.0%
	5.2 Schedule the accounting and administrative controls.	0.0%
	5.3 Identify management reports/indicators.	0.0%
	5.4 Schedule audits.	50.0%
	5.5 Define continuity management and risk controls.	80.0%
	5.6 Identify the resources required by controls and audits.	60.0%

Table 7.8
Activities related to the administrative and control unit's planning

4. Based on the progress of the activities, estimate the process consistency. Do it by determining the geometric average[90] of the activities' progresses, as stated in Formula 7.9

$$\%\,\text{CONSISTENCY}_{\text{PROCESS}} = \left((1+\text{PROGRESS}_1\,\%) \times (1+\text{PROGRESS}_2\,\%) \times .. (1+\text{PROGRESS}_n\,\%) \right)^{(1/n)} - 1$$

Formula 7.9
Formula to calculate Consistency.

Based on the calculation, Consistency represents the progress of the exercises (i.e., activities) that make it possible to complete our strategic plan processes. In our example, consistency reached 40.41%.

This is not an exact measurement since the activities' execution thoroughness must be "incorporated" in their progress assessment. Likewise, the relative importance of each activity to complete each process is ignored, which undermines the formula accuracy.

[90] We use the geometric mean since it is less sensitive to extreme values, although its statistical significance is lower than that obtained from the arithmetic mean.

Despite all omissions, the fact of considering the progress of the activities related to each process is a very constructive exercise. Remember that our aim is to understand if our strategic stage's processes are preceded by the execution of other exercises that offer truthful evidence and information that increases the reliability of our overall strategy.

7.5 Other indicators

From the Progress and Consistency indices, it is possible to create other indicators that reveal the quality and risk related to our entrepreneurial exercise. Here, we refer to "Integrity" and "Risk Level".

Those two indicators are not infallible metrics, but very useful in our evaluation tests, when entrepreneurs have interacted with our Entrepreview® platform.

Because of their importance in controlling entrepreneurship exercises, let us review their meaning and scope.

a. Integrity

Integrity is a metric that rates how "complete" the execution of the strategic stage is. This condition combines the progress of a process with the reliability provided by previously accomplished exercises that offer relevant information and evidence.

We calculate it through the arithmetic product between the progress of the process itself and its consistency degree, both expressed in percentage terms, as suggested by equation 7.10.

$$\%\ \text{INTEGRITY}_{\text{PROCESS}} = \%\ \text{CONSISTENCY} \times \%\ \text{PROGRESS}$$

Equation 7.10
Integrity calculation formula

Regarding its calculation, this metric inherits the deficiencies of the progress and consistency indicators. However, it shows how "representative" is the process of the scrutinized reality, and its "significance" in the decision on whether to launch the business.[91].

To illustrate the calculation, Matrix 7.11 presents the assessment of the Integrity achieved by the eight activities that comprise an unspecific process.

Progress and consistency	Progress (20% 40% 60% 80% 100%)	Consistency	Integrity
1. Define the forecast's horizon and frequency		100%	100%
2. Define business conditions and contexts		60%	36%
3. Project revenue and other income		40%	16%
4. Calculate direct costs		30%	12%
5. Identify expenses		45%	36%
6. Determine margins and break-even points		33%	7%
7. Budget the assets cost		55%	33%
8. Quantify possible contributions and loans		65%	52%
Averages	**63%**	**54%**	**36%**

Matrix 7.11

Matrix of progress and consistency to estimate integrity of a process.

As shown, a 100% integrity refers the completed execution of the tasks included in each activity, with a 100% of consistency (See activity No. 1) [92].

An intermediate integrity values for the rest of the activities may be more or less acceptable to conclude the exercise.

To understand when integrity is "acceptable", Entrepreview® establishes ranges that corelate integrity to the risk level. These thresholds are shown on Table 7.12.

Integrity ranges		
100% - 85%	High integrity	Low risk level
84% - 60%	Medium integrity	High risk level
59% - 30%	Low integrity	Highest risk level
Less than 30%	Incipient project	

Table 7.12

Risk level as a function of Integrity ranges

91 In the Entrepreview® trails, users have endorsed this index usefulness.

92 This is not the most common condition, especially when we undertake complex projects, or starting up businesses in no transparency contexts.

For integrity values that seem acceptable (i.e. 84%-60%), risk levels are significant. Keep in mind that the last objectives of the strategic phase (i.e., financial valuation and financing), are usually incomplete for these progress levels, which makes the decision to launch the business questionable.

Only for integrity values that match the first range (i.e. higher than 84%), it is recommended to decide if we should continue with the pre-operational stage.

As can see, this scale for qualifying risks doesn't seem gradual and may even be discretionary. However, let's remember that metrics seek to conservatively rate the risk conditions arising from an incomplete planning exercises. Here we perfectly achieved this purpose.

b. Risk level

Another factor to determine is the "Risk Level". This variable, critical in any business analysis, represents the exposure to events because of the strategic stage omissions.

Based on the logic to define Integrity, Risk Level represents how many things we didn't consider in our business planning. Therefore, we calculate the work to be done as the complement of the Integrity, as stated in Equation 7.13.

$$\%\ \text{RISK LEVEL}_{\text{PROCESS}} = 100\% - \%\ \text{INTEGRITY}$$

Equation 7.13
Formula to estimate the level of risk of a process

The key to understand this relationship is to consider the volume of data we need to make less risky business decisions. The greater the number of factors we analyze, the better supported and complete our planning will be.

As we have seen, both attributes hand in hand with higher integrity. But they also represent the flexibility to handle the uncertainty of organizing and running a business.

Here we are not talking about any flexibility. We refer to the ability to react to changes in conditions that we considered in our strategic exercise. The idea is to prepare answers, according to the available resources, aligned with the goals that we have set.

This is the type of planning that reduces uncertainties and offers more security when making our business decision.

In our opinion, the exposed indicators are valid options for entrepreneurs to measure the reliability of their analyzes and conclusions. In fact, the tests we've run on Entrepreview® suggest a strong correlation between the level of risk measured in these terms and the mortality rate of the new business.

Despite the findings, we continue to improve analyzes, including new variables. For now, we invite you to consider these indexes that help make comparisons that match the common sense.

7.6 Sources of risk

During the strategic phase, we must get information to improve our criteria and increase the security margin to develop a sustainable project.

We have maintained that the execution of this initial phase must be as complete as possible. If we do not achieve this condition, we would develop a business with unresolved sources of risk that will become in omissions, inconsistencies and errors that would cause delays, higher costs, and additional risk sources.

As a product of the link between planning and sources of risk, we have solid evidence of the relationship between the execution of each strategic process and the sources of risk that may be created.

This finding offers the possibility of anticipating problems derived from our omissions, which create a very effective work map to complete our planning process.

Because of this clear-cut link, we can create guides that show the cause-effect relationship mentioned here. See an example in Table 7.14, where we analyze, the processes comprising the objective of "Managing financing".

Risk analysis
(Hotel and hospitality businesses)

Risk analysis

1 Business idea feasibility

REMARK: If this objective is not fully met, the future business would lack of references to establish its physical, managerial and financial dimensions. It's also possible to disregard the real barriers or restrictions that could condition the business performance. Both would make it difficult to define the acceptable risk threshold for founders.

Processes

1 Define the Key Concepts of Entrepreneurship.
2 Study the product manufacture feasibility.
3 Identify Formal and legal Duties.

If processes are omitted or improperly completed, it would affect the same entrepreneurship exercise, creating sources of risk that would expose the new business to the occurrence of events that would involve different losses.

Weakness or potential source of risk
No clear business definition
Lack of goals and objectives
The legal framework is unknown
Formalities to fulfill are not identified
No budget for formal duties
No prepared documentation to request licenses and permits
Failure to comply with tax and employer formalities
No facility with conditions to provide the service
There is no comprehensive security system
Goals do not respond to the accommodation capacity
Lack of definition of priority areas

Potential events
Over or underinvestment of resources
Delays or failure to meet goals
Inability to provide complementary services
Fines and closures
Customer complaints
Inability to fully operate
Cancellation of the undertaking
Robberies, theft and lost

Potential impacts on future business
Loss because of illiquidity
Loss of funding sources
Loss of corporative image

Table 7.14
Risk sources and their potential events
Objective: Financing management

This type of report is very useful, not only for understanding the reason for every process. It also offers references about the quality of the work required to reduce the entrepreneurship risk.[93].In this way, the sections comprising the analysis are the following:

1. The objective under analysis.
2. Processes comprising the objective.
3. Potential shortcomings to face if we do not meet the objective.
4. Sources of risk produced by the omission or poor processes execution.
5. Events that typically stem from the risk sources.
6. Potential impacts identified according to the chapter two classification.

93 In Attachment D shows all risk matrices corresponding to the planning of a lodging service (Hotels).

Entrepreneurs can always reorder, rename, breakdown, or even increase the number of processes in their strategic work plan. However, to identify the whole risks universe, we recommend not to omit any processes.

Please consider there is no redundancy along the fifteen processes and their seventy-five activities. Therefore, if we do not complete any activity, it would mean that some critical information, report, or evidence will not exist. This may affect the reliability of the strategic phase, the execution of the pre-operational phase, or both.

i! Entrepreview®

Building tables to orderly make the suggested calculations, is not a simple task. Entrepreview® makes these calculations, converts them into analysis tables and uses them to identify the risk sources to effectively control risks.

Indeed, the information gaps can be addressed by assuming unverified information. Hence, we make calculations that use variables we take for granted because informal sources or our common sense suggest it.

However, when this practice becomes extreme, adopting variables linked to the value creation (e.g., sales prices), lead to a reduction in our planning reliability.

Keep in mind that these "oversights" deteriorate the entrepreneurship reliability in the eyes of those interested in reviewing our work. Consequently, the more we focus on supporting our planning and valuation with solid evidence, the greater certainty we will offer to all those who invest their assets in the new project, among others, your-self.

7.7 The work plan (a summary)

Before concluding, it is useful to review the steps for monitoring and controlling your planning, now considering the indicators explained. The order we suggest is the following:

1. Supplement the task list you have prepared, with the activities suggested here to complete your planning process. (See Tables Attachment A). If required, create additional lists to merge them without skipping activities that may provide essential information.

2. Based on the activities list, you must prepare a list of resources, sources of information, or experts for the completion of each activity. Believe it or not, keeping an appointments schedule makes the task ahead much easier.

3. As far as possible, establish an order in which to carry out your strategic phase. To do this, you can create a tentative schedule that does not omit pending tasks or activities (See Schedule in Attachment F.1).

4. Design a table that allows tracking your work, identifying the progress made in each activity or process (See Table in Attachment F.2). Make your notes on it, to not forget useful details. Progressively, you will determine the consistency and progress achieved.

5. For those unfinished processes (because of doubts or lack of knowledge), we recommend consulting Attachment D matrices that show the events that may occur if we do not address the corresponding risk sources. This revision creates a fresh approach to the processes that make their execution much easier.

Finally, use your common sense and don't stop criticizing your work. Ask questions. Be exhaustive by researching and comparing. Take your business seriously. All the effort you invest in your initiative will be reversed in your favor. Make efforts to achieve excellence in your work. You and your business idea are well worth it.

¡Good luck in your entrepreneurship!

8. Attachments

Attachment A. Strategic phase's process and activities

Legal / technical / commercial feasibility

Pre evaluation	• Define the business concept. • Identify the reasons to promote an entrepreneurship. • Identify the business key elements. • Determine the Entrepreneurship success Factors. • Establish the business Mission and Objectives.
Manufacturing feasibility	• Draw up a sketch / blueprint of the product (s). • Create or access recipe / formula / manufacturing process. • Define the packaging and presentation of the product. • Confirm access / availability to the required resources • Elaborate a prototype / product sample.
Formalities and compliance	• Review the legal and regulatory framework • Identify the compliance / registrations / licenses required • Identify the control entities. • Identify processes, information and documents required. • Schedule formalities/duties to fulfill in the future.

Table A.1
List of the activities that comprise the strategic stage objective 1 processes.

Design of Operation Model

Planning the Productive Process	• Identify Production/Manufacturing Process steps. • Identify machinery, equipment, and tools to manufacturing. • Quantify raw material consumption, inventories and waste material. • Establish conditions that facility must be met. • Define the required maintenance and industrial safety plan.
Planning the Business Administration and Control	• Identify/schedule the necessary/required business controls. • Identify the Management Reports to create and submit. • Schedule the Audits to be performed. • Define Business Continuity Management and Risk Control plans. • Identify the resources to controls and audit.
Planning the staff and its managing	• Define the number and employees' role in each area. • Establish professional profile/experience for every position. • Define salaries and payroll benefits. • Plan recruiting, selecting, and hiring staff processes. • Establish policies to manage and commit the staff.

Table A.2
List of the activities that comprise the strategic stage objective 2 processes.

Designing a Marketing Plan

Positioning the Product	• Define the market and identify its dimensions and barriers. • Segment the market, defining niches and participants. • Predefine the potential consumer profile and preferences. • Define the market research. • Carry the research out and confirm the customer and preferences.
Sales and Distribution Model	• Identify/select the sales model. • Identify participants of sales network. • Define the selling model through social media and Internet. • Evaluate the distribution/delivery channels. • Define the legal/duties to make commercial agreements
Advertising and Promotion plans	• Evaluate the advertising/promotional plans convenience. • Define the advertising plan's objectives and content. • Determine cost/scope of advertising/promotional plans. • Determine the advertising/promotional plan costs/conditions • Schedule the advertising/promotional plans.

Table A.3
List of the activities that comprise the strategic stage objective 3 processes.

Establishing Financial Feasibility

Forecasting the incomings	• Define the price/quality ratio of the product(s). • Compare price/quality ratio with competitors. • Set the sales goals based on initial demand and business strategy. • Define prices, expenses, and receivables for distribution channels. • Forecast the potential revenues and receivable accounts.
Forecasting the outgoings	• Forecast the direct and indirect costs of production. • Forecast the assets and other resources purchases. • Define the most likely production volume to estimate the unitary cost. • Set the payment and discounts terms from suppliers. • Forecast the cash outflows and the payable accounts.
Business valuation	• Carry out a strategic SWOT analysis and develop a business plan • Elaborate an incoming and outgoings budget • Establish a cash flows forecast. • Identify the cash deficit/surplus and required funding. • Determine an equity value.

Table A.4
List of the activities that comprise the strategic stage objective 4 processes.

Society foundation

Conditions for funding	• Set the convenience/possibility to fund the project on your own. • Identify the available partners/lenders to fund the business. • Identify the steps to access each funding source. • Determine the funding impact on profitability and business control • Contact potential partners/lenders to confirm their interest.
Planning negotiations	• Plan the meeting's agenda with each partner/lender. • Prepare a Business Plan. • Design the presentation of the Business plan. • Prepare a Value Proposition. • Prepare different options for negotiations.
Partnership's constitution	• Define the memorandum of association. • Designate the partners. • Approve the Financial Statements. • Appoint the Board of Directors and legal representatives. • Register the company's memorandum of association.

Table A.5
List of the activities that comprise the strategic stage objective 5 processes.

Attachment B. Preoperative phase's processes and activities

Processes	Activities
Administration and Control	• Assume/delegate the accounting duties. • Bank accounts administration. • Organize procurement processes, payroll and service payments, clearance and collections. • Prepare and distribute management reports, records and files.
License processing and fulfilling formal duties	• Organize/perform formal duties. • Collect documents and supports for each duty. • Budget the formal duties costs. • Proceed to request permits, certificates and licenses. • Activate insurance coverage for premises, equipment and staff.
Selection and formal possession of local/facilities	• Identify suitable facilities to build the business. • Negotiate the acquisition/rental of the selected facility. • Formalize the agreement and make deposits/guarantees. • Comply all legal duties to operate at the facility. • Condition the facility with basic operational/physical security elements.
Acquisition / installation of machines & equipment	• Confirm suppliers' conditions to buy machinery and equipment. • Negotiate purchase and delivery terms. • Transport machinery/equipment. • Install machinery/equipment. • Adjust and test machinery/equipment.
Planning the purchase of raw materials and other supplies	• Define inventories to start and keep production. • Agree with suppliers' prices/quantities/payment. • Issue purchase orders to acquire raw materials and supplies. • Receive supplies, controlling quantities and specifications. • Accounting raw material/supplies received

Processes	Activities
Recruitment and personnel induction	• Start recruitment process. • Receive and evaluate curriculum/candidate summaries. • Post salary and benefits. • Meet formalities to hire employees. • Carry out employees' induction.
Testing and adjusting the production process	• Train personnel to operate machinery and equipment. • Tests supplies/raw material to confirm if meeting specifications. • Test and adjust the manufacturing/packaging process. • Quantify consumption of waste, raw material, and supplies. • Create, store, and register inventories.
Creating the sales channels	• Design guidelines to sell the product(s). • Contact potential customers/retailers/wholesalers sending samples. • Negotiate delivery/price/collection/visibility/location and returns guidelines with retailers and others. • Reprogram production schedule based on the expected sales
Distribution and delivery channels setting up	• Determine the distribution logistic and outsourcings. • Acquire/hire transportation to deliver goods/products. • Make contracts that formalize commercial agreements. • Quantify/compare the distribution/delivery cost/times. • Adjust plan production based on delivery capacity.
Implementing an Advertising / Promotion Plan	• Hire/undertake the advertising plan launching. • Establish content, forms, and means to advertise. • Measure the advertising plan effect on sales • Planning promotions with retailers/wholesalers • Measure the promotion effect on sales

Attachment C. Business areas' processes and activities.

Case (Manufacturing business)

Families	Processes	Activities
ADMINISTRATION AND COMPTROLLER: Includes all the administrative, support and control activities to manage the organization	**Accounting and financial registrations**	• Administration of account codes. • Accounting record of operations. • Custody of supports, invoices and records.
	Collection, processing and internal/external information submission	• Preparation of the financial statements. • Creation and use of management indicators. • Databases aadministration.
	Audit of activities, records and resources	• Definition/execution of audit plans/comptroller. • Control of cases and events. • Supervision of legal duties compliance.
OPERATION AND PRODUCTION: Includes the necessary operations that provide a service or manufacture a product	**Execution of operations**	• Execution of business-as-usual activities. • Registration, control and support of operations. • Report of the business performance/outcome.
	Inventory Management	• Purchase and supplies reception. • Control of products in process' inventories. • Handling finished products.
	Application of technical and labor standards	• Update and application of technical standards. • Control of work capacity and technique. • Quality control setup.
Assets management: Includes endowing the business with resources that make possible its productive processes.	**Acquisition of equipment / machinery**	• Supervision and suppliers' management. • Identification of equipment/machines. • Purchase equipment, machinery and tools.
	Maintenance	• Setup/follow up a maintenance plan. • Acquisition of parts, spares and other supplies. • Execution of maintenance/repairments plan.
	Other assets management	• Administration and assets control. • Valuation and assets appraisal. • Protection and fixed assets maintenance.
PERONNEL MANAGEMENT: Includes activities that make effective the staff management.	**Recruitment and induction**	• Staff selection and hiring. • Induction and personnel training. • Benchmarking of salaries and other benefits.
	Training and talent development	• Design of training plans. • Evaluation and suppliers' control. • Monitoring and evaluation of the career plans.
	Payroll management and employer formal duties	• Payroll administration. • Managing compensation and benefits. • Payment of fiscal/parafiscal obligations.

Families	Processes	Activities
TRADING AND MARKET RELATIONS : Includes the policies of transactions with suppliers, customers, and other counterparties.	**Commercial relationship with suppliers**	• Purchase of goods/supplies (local or import). • Managing the relationship with suppliers. • Administration of alliances/agreements.
	Commercial relationship with customers	• Provision of the service, sale or export. • Management of marketing and sales plans. • Administration of commercial agreements.
	Monitoring competition	• Monitoring the market and its participants. • Managing the market share. • Establishing strategic alliances or partnerships.
LEGAL PROCESS: Includes all laws and regulations compliance, as well as the administration of any legal processes/relations that involve the business.	**Fulfillment formal duties**	• Attend administrative processes in control entities. • Deliver information regularly to the control entities. • Adjust the company activity to the legal framework.
	Monitoring legal processes	• Care complaints against the company. • Support formal issues that involve the business. • Assistance to trials or legal processes.
	Third party's relations	• Drafting and negotiating contracts. • Legalize commercial and financial agreements. • Represent the company before any third party.
FINANCIAL OPERATIONS: Includes the plans and operations to efficiently manage the deficits and surplus cash, as well as the credits that fund the bsuiness.	**Cash management**	• Monitoring and management of cash flow • Investment portfolio management • Distribution of information and reports
	Funding	• Evaluation of financing alternatives • Fulfillment of duties and formalities • Schedule the financing's repayment
	Granting of credits	• Identifying conditions to grant credits to customers • Evaluation of the client's financial status • Planning the credits collection
STRATEGIC PLANNING: Includes the definition, diffusion, and execution of strategies to sustain or improve the business competitiveness	**Definition of goals and objectives**	• SWOT Analysis • Definition of short-, medium- and long-term objectives • Preparation of business plans
	Dissemination and implementation of plans	• Definition of strategies • Formulation of budgets • Coordination of work plans
	Measurement of results and feedback	• Results monitoring and goals comparison • Plan/correction setting up • Planning risk control

Families	Processes	Activities
ENVIRONMENTS AFFAIRS Include the set of must-comply conditions to protect business from any natural event, and the environmental carefulness to accomplish a sustainable activity	**Coverage for natural events and accidents**	• Design of a secure headquarters • Installation of warning systems • Acquisition of insurance policies / coverage contracts
	Environmental Protection	• Adopt a rational consumption of resources • Establish efficient waste management • Promotion of recycling programs
PUBLIC AFFAIRS Includes any action that prevents, mitigate, or transfer the effects from criminal events. Also, the management of the business image and its public relations.	**Surveillance and protection against crime**	• Installation / adoption of systems / security standards • Physical protection of the facility and headquarters • Protection of computer systems against hacking
	Public opinion and institutional relationships	• Establish links with public and private entities • Promote institutional advertising campaigns • Promote or contribute with humanitarian social initiatives

Attachment D. Risk matrices

Risk analysis
(Hotel and hospitality businesses)

Risk analysis

1 Business idea feasibility

REMARK: If this objective is not fully met, the future business would lack of references to establish its physical, managerial and financial dimensions. It's also possible to disregard the real barriers or restrictions that could condition the business performance. Both would make it difficult to define the acceptable risk threshold for founders.

Processes

1 Define the Key Concepts of Entrepreneurship.
2 Study the product manufacture feasibility.
3 Identify Formal and legal Duties.

If processes are omitted or improperly completed, it would affect the same entrepreneurship exercise, creating sources of risk that would expose the new business to the occurrence of events that would involve different losses.

Weakness or potential source of risk	Potential events
No clear business definition	Over or underinvestment of resources
Lack of goals and objectives	Delays or failure to meet goals
The legal framework is unknown	Inability to provide complementary services
Formalities to fulfill are not identified	Fines and closures
No budget for formal duties	Customer complaints
No prepared documentation to request licenses and permits	Inability to fully operate
Failure to comply with tax and employer formalities	Cancellation of the undertaking
No facility with conditions to provide the service	Robberies, theft and lost
There is no comprehensive security system	
Goals do not respond to the accommodation capacity	**Potential impacts on future business**
Lack of definition of priority areas	Loss because of illiquidity
	Loss of funding sources
	Loss of corporative image

Table D.1
Risk sources and their potential events
Objective: Business idea feasibility

Risk analysis
(Hotel and hospitality businesses)

Risk analysis

2 Business operation planning

REMARK: If this objective is not fully met, it would not be possible to establish all the resources that make possible the business operations. It would be difficult to manage it according to the established planning, to track results and maintain control over the sources of risk.

Processes

4 Plan the business operation.
5 Plan the Administration and Control.
6 Plan the Human Work Team.

If processes are omitted or improperly completed, it would affect the same entrepreneurship exercise, creating sources of risk that would expose the new business to the occurrence of events that would involve different losses.

Weakness or potential source of risk	Potential events
Poor serviceability design	Over or underinvestment of resources
Incomplete accounting of the operation	Robberies, theft and installation damages
Uncompetitive salaries	Lack of resources to operate at full capacity
Lack of staff to attend to business areas	Unanticipated cash deficit
Unreal budgets	Fines and closures
Lack of risk control management	High staff turnover
Not planning the profile and number of employees required	Clients complaints
Lack of critical areas definition	High labor absence
Lack of reliable management indicators	
Inconsistency between goals, resources and productive capac	**Potential impacts on future business**
Hire inexperienced staff	Loss because of illiquidity
Manage an incomplete administrative system	Loss of funding sources
	Market share loss

Table D.2
Risk sources and their potential events
Objective: Operation model design

Risk analysis
(Hotel and hospitality businesses)

Risk analysis

3 **Marketing plan**

REMARKS: If this objective is not fully met, it is possible to deviate the efforts to serve customers who are willing/need to consume our product/service. Business opportunities can be missed, but also overspending our advertising, offering our service to the wrong group of consumers.

Processes

7 Identify the market, its niches and the consumer.
8 Plan the sales and distribution model.
9 Plan advertising and promotion.

If processes are omitted or improperly completed, it would affect the same entrepreneurship exercise, creating sources of risk that would expose the new business to the occurrence of events that would involve different losses.

Weakness or potential source of risk

Potential customer not duly identified
Effective sales channels are not developed
Insufficient budget to advertise
There are no fee policies
No strategy to differentiate from competitors
There is no business' image
Rates are uncompetitive
Promotional plans are not designed/implemented
Competition unknown
No complementary services offered

Potential events

Low occupancy rate
Sales targets not met
Low profit margins
Very expensive promotions
Low customer loyalty
No increasing demand in vacation seasons
Lack of capacity to meet demand

Potential impacts on future business

Loss because of illiquidity
Loss of corporative image

Table D.3
Risk sources and their potential events
Objective: Marketing plan

Risk analysis
(Hotel and hospitality businesses)

Risk analysis

4 **Financial valuation**

REMARKS: If this objective is not fully met, we could not determine the equity value of our project. It prevents to understand the convenience of launching our new business following a well-designed strategy. Ignoring the value also prevents a fair association with third parties.

Processes

10 Calculate and project inflows.
11 Calculate and project outflows.
12 Evaluate the project.

If processes are omitted or improperly completed, it would affect the same entrepreneurship exercise, creating sources of risk that would expose the new business to the occurrence of events that would involve different losses.

Weakness or potential source of risk

Unknown business strategy
Difficulties to define the scale of the service
Fares are not based on an accurate unit cost
Cash deficits cannot be foreseen.
Potential insufficiencies since a lack of suppliers' payment po
Insufficient funding because of no investment budget.
Fares do not respond to the cost structure
No sales goals
There are no convenient collection policies
Critical areas are unknown

Potential events

Over or underinvestment of resources
Insufficient funding
Under/over leveraging the company
Low sales
Unscheduled tax charges
Unprofitable operation or lose money
Unanticipated cash deficit
Unequal partnership

Potential impacts on future business

Profit margin loss
Loss of funding sources
Loss because of illiquidity
Loss of corporative image

Table D.4
Risk sources and their potential events
Objective: Financial valuation

Risk analysis
(Hotel and hospitality businesses)

Risk analysis

5 **Financing management**

REMARKS: If this objective is not fully met, the business would not have access to financing sources consistent with its needs and its repayment capabilities. Likewise, there is a risk of establishing a partnership without protecting founders shareholding.

Processes

13 Evaluate financing conditions.
14 Plan the negotiation with each source of financing.
15 Establish the Company.

If processes are omitted or improperly completed, it would affect the same entrepreneurship exercise, creating sources of risk that would expose the new business to the occurrence of events that would involve different losses.

Weakness or potential source of risk

No information on required financing
Financing costs unknown
No documentation to apply for a credit
No information to define a value proposition
Lack of a well-capitalized company
No value's reference to sell equity
No business strategy that offers value
Lack of a legal company representative
Lack of formal mechanisms to manage the partnership
Lack of guarantees to support a financing
There is no business plan

Potential events

Partners disagreements
Not get the financing required
No formal association with third parties
No financing for future business stages
Impossibility of achieving the business scale
Postpone/cancel entrepreneurship
Dilute the entrepreneur shareholding

Potential impacts on future business

Loss because of illiquidity
Loss of corporative image
Loss of funding sources

Table D.5
Risk sources and their potential events
Objective: Financing management

Attachment E. Matrices gallery

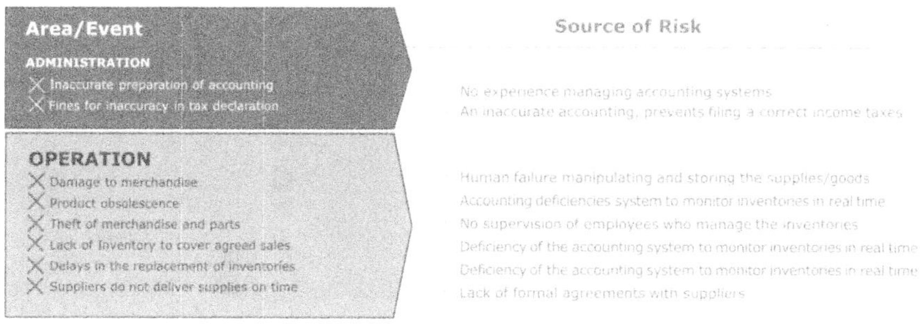

Matrix A. Areas-Events-Risk sources

Processes of two different areas are under analysis. Here, the events that occurred in a food marketing company are correlated with their sources of risk.

	Personnel			Organization			Assets			Information						
	Qualified	Sufficient	Committed	Relevant	Updated	Diffused	Available	Maintened	Safety	Effective	Efficient	Confidential	Integral	Available	Legal	Reliable
Reception documents/information		x		x												
Revision documents/information	x			x	x											
Rating borrower profile	x			x								x	x		x	x
Credit approval	x															
Client's credit acceptance												x				
Registration of the credit in the system	x															
Loan contract formalization	x	x			x									x	x	
Credit in the customer's bank account		x					x									

The official that review the application and the applicant's profile must be well-experience to establish risk profile.

The credit applicant must be fully informed of the documents and information to submit

There must be a comprehensive technical and administrative procedure to verify the applicant information

The applicants' information must be true and sufficient to determine its credit scoring according to the existing regulations

Credit agreements must consider all conditions previously agreed with the applicants

Matrix B. Areas-Risk sources

Relevant sources of risk in the activities involved in a line of credit granting. This matrix is useful for specifying lack of each activity under control.

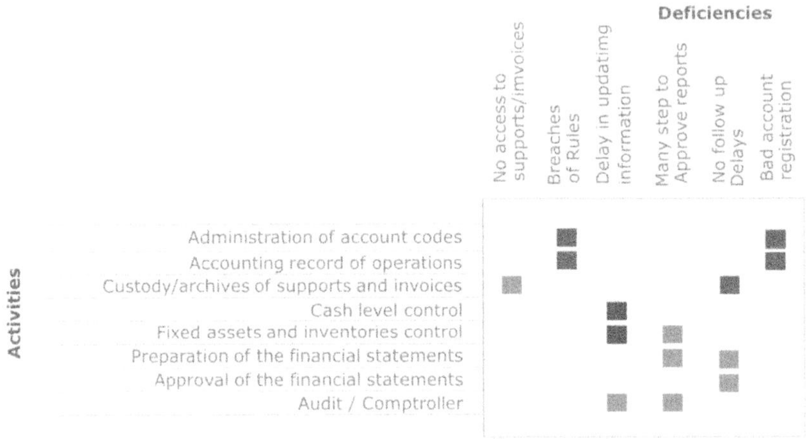

Matrix C. Areas-Risk sources

Analysis of a manufacturing company's critical areas. Risk sources are identified and ranked (see numbering) according to their potential impact.

RESOURCES/SOURCES OF RISK

AREAS	PERSONNEL	ORGANIZATION	INFORMATION	OTHER ASSETS
Administration			6	
Operation		4		
Trading	3	3		
Staff Management		5		
Planning		7	7	
Asset management	2	2		
Public opinión affairs	1			

1 There are no security guards on the factory premises, nor security company to delegate on these duties (i.e., lack of personnel)

2 There is no procedure to purchase (import) parts and spares to maintain the machinery. The main plastic injector has stopped working for prolonged periods. (i.e., staff and follow-up missing)

3 There is no marketing manager to reposition the products lines. Today the company concentrates 85% of the sales on three clients, which fosters a risky dependency. (i.e., personnel to control sales and operations is missing)

4 Production plan is continuously changed because of products orders changes. Unscheduled changes mean delays in manufacture and sale. (i.e., lack of management guidelines)

5 The current Human Resources management has not designed an incentiva plan to increases the key employees' commitment, among others: machine operators and production managers (i.e., management guidelines are missing)

6 Accounting system deficiencies to monitor inventories in real time. The inventories control module is incomplete and does not adapt to the management guidelines. Therefore, the controls are carried in alternate manual registers. (i.e., lack of administrative systems)

7 The planning of the company is nor supported on complete and updated information. Many reports and accounting information do not exist or are not submitted timely. (i.e., lack of capacity to produce and distribute information)

Matrix D. Areas-Deficiencies

List of deficiencies identified in the activities comprises a health service company administrative area. Here, criticality grade is based on colors.

DEFICIENCIES	POTENTIAL EVENTS	PRIORITY
Delay units' maintenance	Additional repairments and costs	4
Parts purchase orders are processed late	No prices' reductions from greater spare/parts purchasing	5
Communication equipment have limited reach	Increase safety problems for drivers	2
Taximeters are not installed in all units	No operating costs control	6
Drivers meet restricted schedules	Less alternatives to increase revenues	3
There is no reliable workshop to repair units	Larger out-of-duty units' lapse	1

Matrix E. Deficiencies-Events
The matrix relates the taxis company operational deficiencies, with events that could lead losses for the company. Events are ranked by importance, which offers a useful guide to control the weaknesses detected.

Areas	Severity	Potential critical event (example)
Administration/Comptroller	A	Loss of financial/accounting information
Assets management	C	Employees stealing the inventory
Environmental affairs	B	Delay in garbage collection
Public opinion affairs	C	Physical damage on consumers
Operations and production	D	Inadequate refrigeration of product/supplies
Market position	C	Lose attractive to the customers
Financial operations	E	Cash deficit
Strategic planning	C	Biased or incomplete planning
Personnel management	D	High turnover of personnel
Legal duties	C	No timely tax return filing

Matrix F. Areas-Severity-Critical potential event.
A list of the critical events that may occur at the restaurant operation areas. Ranking of potential events is based on letters.

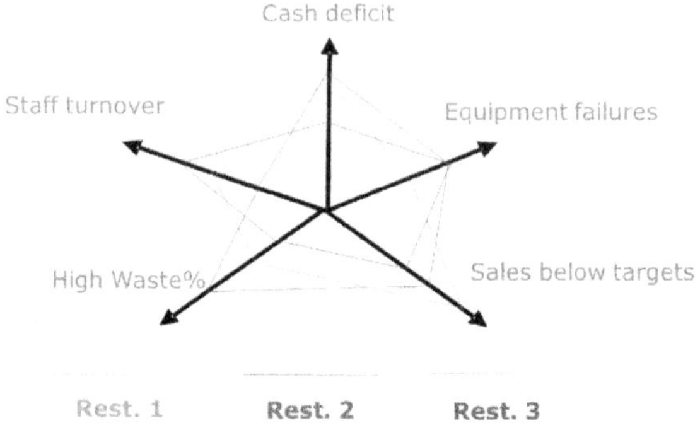

Matrix G. Severity.
This matrix compares losses of three branches of a restaurant chain, based on the five most common events.

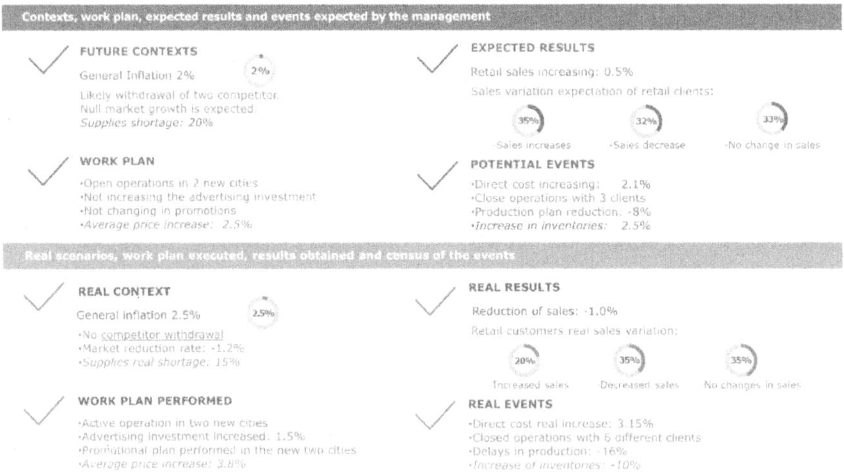

Matrix H. Contexts – Events.
A manufacturer of toiletries designed a work plan that assumed different contexts. Its goals are compared with the results obtained

Attachment F. Work-flow control matrices

Process/Activity — Weeks

1 2 3 4 5 6 7 8 9 10

PRE EVALUATION
- Basic business concept.
- Reasons to inititate a new business.
- Business key elements.
- Entrepreneurship success cactors.
- Business mission and objectives.

MANUFACTURING FEASIBILITY
- Sketch/blueprint of the product.
- Create or access recipe/formula/manufacturing process.
- Define the packaging and presentation.
- Confirm acces /availability of resources
- Elaborate a prototype/sample.

FORMALITIES AND COMPLIANCE
- Review the current legal and regulatory framework
- Identify compliance/registrations/licenses.
- Identify control entities.
- Identify formal processes and documentation.
- Schedule futures formal duties.

Schedule F.1
Execution plan of the activities of three processes that determine the "business viability". Manufacturing company case.

Process/Activities — % Progress

20% 40% 60% 80% 100%

PRE EVALUATION 90%
- Basic business concept.
- Reasons to inititate a new business.
- Business key elements.
- Entrepreneurship success cactors.
- Business mission and objectives.

MANUFACTURING FEASIBILITY 60%
- Sketch/blueprint of the product.
- Create or access recipe/formula/manufacturing process.
- Define the packaging and presentation.
- Confirm acces /availability of resources
- Elaborate a prototype/sample.

FORMALITIES AND COMPLIANCE 60%
- Review the current legal and regulatory framework
- Identify compliance/registrations/licenses.
- Identify control entities.
- Identify formal processes and documentation.
- Schedule futures formal duties.

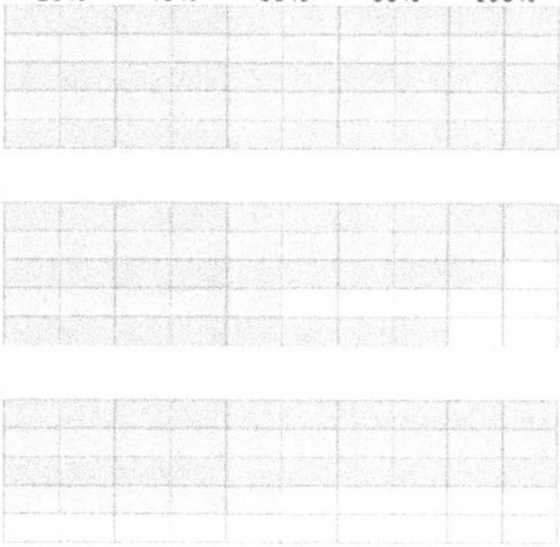

Table F.2
Progress degree of the "feasibility of the business" processes. The progress would be those achieved 6 weeks after initiating the activities planned through schedule F.1.

Made in the USA
Monee, IL
04 November 2026

67387469R10075